The Story So Far

The Story So Far

We all have a purpose in life,
a reason to be; sometimes we
have to find it for ourselves

Vivienne Boulton

authorHOUSE®

AuthorHouse™ UK Ltd.
1663 Liberty Drive
Bloomington, IN 47403 USA
www.authorhouse.co.uk
Phone: 0800.197.4150

Published by AuthorHouse   04/22/2014

ISBN: 978-1-4772-4579-8 (sc)
ISBN: 978-1-4772-4580-4 (e)

Chapters

Inspiration

My mother wrote a small book called Reflections by J. Rawson. She was no writer. She wanted to put down on paper, memories of her younger life for others to read about.

Book References

Reflections by J. Rawson

The Power of Your Subconscious Mind by Dr. Joseph Murphy,P,H,D,D,D (Revised by Ian McMchan, Ph.D.)

The Power of Now by Eckhart Tolle

Anti-Cancer, A new way of life by Dr David Servan-Schreiber.

Epigenetics—The Genie in your Genes, Dawson Church PhD.

Quantum Change by William R. Miller and Janet C'de Baca

Love Medicine and Miracles by Bernie Siegal

The Love Affair

December 1996

It was New Year's Eve. I was feeling good and excited at the prospect of a great evening with friends. We were at a lovely hotel near where we lived. It always did a great social function, especially New Year's Eve! It is 16th Century, oak beams, full of charm and ambiance, great food, entertainment and plenty of dancing till late. As my husband and I entered the bar area, complete with parrot in cage, open inglenook fire and piano, I saw two of my friends at the bar chatting and smiling, glasses in their hands. "Hi Tony," I said, as I smiled and gave him a peck on the cheek. I turned to look at Roger and touched his arm lightly with my hand as I kissed him too. "You look like a nice young man!" I gaily said. He smiled back and thought to himself 'this is going to be a fun evening'.

Off I went to join the other wives and soon there were eight of us drinking cocktails and getting in the mood for fun. The restaurant was packed. It was always a great night at this hotel on New Year's Eve. Everyone dressed up for the occasion, the men in evening gear, the ladies in their fabulous dresses. Everyone was intent on making it a night to remember. The dinner was wonderful with sparkling conversation and banter going back and forth across the table. I sat opposite Roger and was feeling flirty and full of mischief. There was something very warm about his smile. What gorgeous eyes he had! Funny I hadn't noticed them before. We chatted and smiled along with everyone else, but there did seem to be a magnetism between us that night. I felt compelled to flirt with him, and after the meal, over coffee and liqueurs, our attention to each other excluded the others, our eyes meeting and lingering. It was beginning to get a grip of us both. Suddenly we were distracted by the others' laughter and the spell was broken.

Everyone was in party mode and at 12 o'clock it was a riot of streamers, silly string, balloons and party poppers, lots of kisses and happy new year cheers. Our friends were all feeling the effects of a lot to drink and the place was heaving with people all wishing each other Happy New Year! Little did Roger and I know what effect this evening was going to have on our future.

Later that night Roger went to the bar and as he returned a slow dance was being played. I was sitting at the end of our long table against the wall, chatting across to Karen my best friend who was further down the table. The restaurant was laid out with a table along each side, so there was enough room to dance in the middle, in view of everyone. Roger's wife was already dancing with Karen's husband. Roger was determined to ask me to dance, awkward though it would be not to ask Karen first. However I pre-empted this, and as our eyes locked he quickly signalled me to join him, and I left my seat and moved onto the dance floor. We began to move slowly to the music and our bodies gradually pressed closer together. I liked the touch of him. I felt his hands on my back and moved closer still. We talked into each other's ears. "You smell nice" I said. My face was very close to his and I suddenly thought how it might look to our friends and pulled back. We looked at each other and smiled. At the same time we realised this was a temptation which we were not going to be able to pass up easily. Roger had never been unfaithful to his wife in 20 years despite many opportunities with his bachelor lifestyle as a rugby touring fanatic. I too had never strayed from my adoring husband but this was fast becoming an overwhelming situation neither of us had the power to resist. As we pressed closer together Roger began to feel how attracted to me he was becoming. As the music stopped we prised ourselves apart and tried to pretend nothing had happened as we swapped partners to dance with our other friends, but all the time our thoughts were rushing away focusing on the intense feelings which had suddenly welled up inside us both.

The evening eventually drew to a close and as we gathered our things and said goodnight Roger managed to whisper "I'd like to see you." "So would I" I hissed. The evening had passed without anyone noticing what had begun, but it was to mark the start of the most intense torrid affair which would lead to times of immense happiness and to the depths of despair for both of us.

It was four days later when Roger was off to his friend's to play snooker, and he visited the local off licence for some beer to take. This happened to be near where I lived. At exactly the same time he came out of the off licence, I was coming round the corner to buy some eggs to bake a cake with my children. Roger came out of the shop carrying a box of beer. He nearly dropped it with shock as we walked towards each other. I was very surprised to see him and my heart began to beat fast. 'Oh no' I thought 'I'm going to have to apologise for my outrageous behaviour on New Year's Eve!' "Hello!" Roger said. I stammered "Hi! You don't normally shop round here do you?" He made an excuse for being there and I started to talk about 'our' New Year's Eve, the other night "We'd had a lot to drink hadn't we? And I said some things I can only apologise for!" Roger said "Well sometimes we say and do things when we are drunk which we might not have the courage to say or do when we are sober." Roger knew this was his chance to take things further. "I'd like to see you again . . . what do you think?" I hesitated and he added—"Tell you what, I'll give you my work number and you could give me a call if you like." I shuffled about while he hurriedly wrote his number on a scrap of paper in his car and he handed it to me. We parted and I folded the paper up very small and slid it into my pocket. It burned a hole there all weekend and I looked at it from time to time wondering if I would ever call it. I took it to work the following Monday and stared at it. I knew I wanted to see him again but the risks involved made me hesitate. I found myself shaking as I dialed his number. He answered the phone. "Hello it's Viv" I said quietly. "Wow, hello!" he said, shocked I had rung and excited at the same time. "I didn't think you'd call." We quickly planned to meet on the Thursday and put the phone down! Phew this was nerve racking stuff. As it happened by the Tuesday, Roger had a meeting booked for him on the Thursday which he could not get out of easily so he nervously rang me at work. "I can't make Thursday now, how about today?" I thought for a few seconds and agreed to meet at 12 o'clock in a quiet little back road nearby. I spent the morning not concentrating on anything at all. Well why not? I said to him, "are you prepared?" He got my drift and stuttered "yes" trying to sound convincing. Now he would have to go to Boots and buy condoms. He hadn't a clue what he needed and felt very awkward just in case he knew someone!

At lunchtime I hurried out to meet him, leapt into the back of his car and laid on the back seat. He sped off and drove out to the woods a few miles away. We giggled and laughed about the events of New Year's Eve, and soon he pulled up at a quiet spot. We got out and started wandering up the path. It was a beautiful winters day, crisp and sunny with a smattering of snow on the fields. We hadn't gone very far along the pathway when he turned to kiss me which he had been wanting to do on New Year's Eve. As he turned towards me I thought 'this is it, if he's not a good kisser I'm out of here!' It was delicious, so soft sensual and lingering, so reinforcing my growing feelings for him. He traced my lips with his finger and electricity flowed between us. We linked hands and walked further up the track. I looked at his hands. I always said you could tell a lot about a man by his hands. They were like a glove to mine. We turned again to kiss and the passion started to rise. We began touching each other. He looked around and saw a fallen tree trunk nearby but before we could make a move towards it a woman appeared around the corner with her dog! This brought us sharply back to reality and we composed ourselves quickly. As we strolled back to the car we held hands and talked. It felt wonderful and we both knew this was merely an interruption to an inevitable end. We were still heady with excitement.

The buzz of such a secretive liaison was gripping and we knew it wouldn't be long until we met again.

For the next few days neither of us could think straight. We were both consumed with thoughts of each other. It was like an addictive drug, and we wanted those feelings again and again. Roger rang me and suggested another meeting. I couldn't wait to see him again. This time we stayed in the car, and this time there were no holds barred! We drove up to a boat yard nearby and frantically touched each other, making love hastily but having the time to realise we were actually doing this. Our first real encounter was mind blowing, and we knew instantly this would not be the last, as our lives were to become more and more entwined. We started seeking out more places to go, and found several off the beaten track, in woods nearby. Once we got out of the car and wandered into some woods, and noticed we were being watched by a pervert! We were very soon out of there, getting severely stung by nettles in our hurry to get away! And another time there seemed to be an interchange of people in cars in a car park, which Roger told me was 'dogging'. How naïve I was.

A little later one of my friends was having a birthday celebration and she decided it would be fun if the eight of us from New Year's Eve got together for a meal at a local pub restaurant. Of course my husband and Roger's wife readily accepted the invitation but Roger and I were very apprehensive about the dinner. What if anyone suspected anything? Could anyone tell what had gone on and what we were thinking? We had our secret and wondered if we would be able to cope with it. The evening arrived and we were very jittery. Roger gulped down two very large Gin and

Tonics at home before walking to the pub. As he and his wife approached the door he was shaking due to a mixture of apprehension and excitement. We all arrived in the bar and Roger and I avoided eye contact. We were seated at the table and Roger was on my left. Richard, Karen's husband was on my right. The conversation was filled with light hearted banter and jokes coming thick and fast. We settled down to a fine meal and lots of wine. Roger and I breathed in each other's smell and if there was an opportunity to brush fingers on the table, or openly pay each other attention we did. It was so exciting. The evening went very quickly and both of us were relieved the evening had gone so well.

The next formal occasion for the group of friends was a few weeks after one of the girl's birthday. This time it was her husband's birthday. Again the eight of us got together at the same restaurant as before. The adrenalin started pumping for us as we met in the bar. We stood close to each other and revelled in the pleasure of it. And so it went on: each private meeting was becoming more risky and each public meeting showed more and more our closeness as our affair developed. And the inevitable happened: one of our friends had seen us being a bit too close for her liking! Karen had noticed the pass and that was the start of a suspicion which was growing and growing. Now my friend was aware of it, she would be looking for it. She was a keen talker and was beginning to take an active role in the scandal. She loved the fact that Roger had proved himself to be the female obsessed cad she thought he was, and would take great pride in furthering the rumours at the slightest opportunity!

A few days after Richard's birthday Karen and I took our kids out for the day when Karen said something rather worrying.

"I've got to tell you! It's to do with Roger. He IS the female chasing bastard everyone thinks he is. He was running his hand up and down my leg, making a pass at me." I was horrified. It was my leg he had been touching! I didn't know what to think! I had heard all this stuff about Roger before we ever met, about how he was a womaniser and when he was away, played away. But here was Karen saying he was trying it on with HER. I told Karen he must be an awful husband and poor Gail, his wife, and was she going to say anything to her own husband. Karen said it was better to keep it to herself or it would cause a rift between the friends. I felt hurt and puzzled. What was he playing at? At the time Roger had actually been away for a few days, and I didn't manage to speak to him until the evening. When he finally called I decided I had to confront him about this. I simply said "I need to ask you something. Is it true that you were running your hand up Karen's legs at her birthday bash?" "What are you talking about?" he exclaimed, "She's making it all up. I never touched her I promise." And after a short pause he slowly said "But I bet I know what has happened. She must have seen me touching your leg, and has tried to cajole you into confessing what I was doing to you by saying I was doing it to her too! Calculating bitch to do that to her best friend"!

The feelings that originally started as lust, passion and desire were changing and developing into something deeper and more meaningful. This was the most intense affair which neither of us could envisage living without. A most stunning affair people only ever read about but it doesn't actually happen in real life. Well it was happening and was all consuming. I was finding I could hardly eat, couldn't sleep, couldn't concentrate, it was very difficult to think about anything else at all really, and Roger felt the same. One day after yet another secret liaison, Roger was about to drive away as I hopped out of his car and into my own, and as I looked across to him he mouthed the words 'I love you', and then shot off. There was no hiding from it, we were in love. I raced back to work, and shaking, I picked up the phone. As he answered I whispered, "I love you too!" He breathed a sigh of relief. There, we had now admitted to feelings too powerful to ignore. We were euphoric. We began to take in the consequences of what it meant to give in to our feelings.

Slowly over the next few weeks and months the feelings grew ever deeper. We took more and more chances, risking our marriages and threatening our stability. One time, after a lunchtime liason, I was heading back to work, and Roger put a tape into my hand, and said to play it when I was on my own. I played it immediately I was in my own car. It was Gene Pitney, Something's Gotten Hold of my Heart. The words were so poignant. It became our tune. He had heard it on the radio and was spellbound by how appropriate it was.

One evening we somehow managed to get a pass and met secretively. I parked my car and we went off to a country pub in Roger's car, where we had a good chance no oned knew us. We were the only ones in there! We had a very nice meal and pretended just for a short while, that this is how it would be like in the future. We went back to the car, and drove till we found a car park which was very dark! We sat in the back, enjoying each other's touch and smell, and were getting quite aroused by the sensory feelings, when suddenly there was a bright torch shone into the rear window, and a policeman's voice saying, "Are you alright in there?". Roger answered firmly "yes thank you", and I responded "we are fine thank you". We sat still and with bated breath. He said" Well if you are sure you are okay I will say goodnight". Phew. That was cold water poured on our fun. We shrieked with laughter when he'd gone. Just our luck, a community policeman on patrol. Still we are all grateful for the service they provide, keeping us safe.

Until one day, for just a few minutes together, the affair was discovered. In a car park, we arranged to meet for a quick hello. Roger walked over and got into my car. He had just leaned across to kiss me when suddenly I heard a car screech to a halt beside mine. I opened my eyes and instantly recognised my husband getting out of his car. What ensued after that was etched in all of our memories for ever. Roger opened the passenger door and got out. Richard began flailing about with fists then took his shirt off, shouting. Roger merely defended himself. I tried to prize them apart but Richard was beside himself with anger. People gathered round as I shouted to them to stop. He got back in his car when he realised he wasn't having it all his own way. He sped off in a flying rage. We were left there stunned and shocked. This was so terrible and was about to get a whole lot worse. He got home and began hurling all my clothes into the garden. This blew things wide open and we had to face the truth. There was no pretending this wasn't happening.

Roger and I gathered ourselves together and hurriedly spoke about what we were going to do and say. There were lots of arguments, discussions, hurt, pain, every emotion touched by this. Roger and I finally got to talk the following day and decided not to get in contact for a while to let things simmer down. But slowly and gradually we began phoning each other and while agreeing about the danger of continuing our love affair, still could not envisage a life without each other. We could not walk away from it, no matter how hard we tried.

But life at home was difficult to deal with. Our partners were continually suspicious and the lies were becoming harder and more complex, but strangely easier to say.

All the while things were growing worse and worse for me. I had decided I knew in my heart who I wanted to be with but the upheaval of breaking up a happy family was too awful to contemplate. Roger seemed to manage his affairs a bit differently and through his charm and ability to smooth the situation over fooled his wife into a false sense of security.

Roger and I were finding it increasingly frustrating finding somewhere to be together and decided it would be ideal to rent somewhere to go to meet up, especially as it had become so frequent by then. We secretly went and viewed suitable properties and took one a few minutes drive away from our homes. It was a charming country terraced house, out of the way. It was ideal for our liaisons. We were so excited and nervous of signing the papers with the rental agency. It made it rather official, and committed on paper, but we did it anyway.

Three months went by and after many rows and a formidable atmosphere I decided I would have to move out. The ideal place would be to the house I rented with Roger and he agreed that if I moved out first he would follow very shortly as Gail would know as soon as Vivienne moved out that Roger would do the same. Richard and I managed to sort things out so that I would take the three girls and he would have them at weekends until things were properly resolved. I told Richard I would look for somewhere to rent and within a couple of weeks had miraculously 'found' a place to rent. He believed me and there followed a horrible weekend of removing things from the marital home down to the new place. The children were really good about the whole thing and were even quite excited at the prospect of moving and have 'two bedrooms each, one at Mummy's and one at Daddy's. It was all like a dream; I felt this could not really be happening to me. Roger and I were constantly on the phone reassuring each other and Roger felt under great pressure to move out of his family home. It took him three weeks before he was ready to go and sadly in this time my husband began to think there was a possible reconciliation. Roger felt it best to move to a hotel for a few days for a cooling off period but in retrospect it didn't make any difference to the hurt and awful emotional trauma that ensued when he moved in with me. Gail was beside herself with grief. She sobbed and sobbed for weeks. She clung to Roger in an hysterical bid to stop him leaving. Richard cried and cried which tore me apart. He begged me not to do this. It was the most traumatic time any of us had ever had and hoped never to have to live through again. Little did either Gail or I especially know our lives were to be torn apart a second time within a few months, for the love of one man.

The weeks went by and things seemed to settle a little for Roger. He constantly reassured Gail he would always be there for her and made valiant efforts to go to their marital home frequently to see her and their children. In fact it appeared to me he was being rather too attentive to them and she was beginning to suffer as a result. Richard grew bitter and resentful very quickly and within a few weeks had begun the process of divorce and financial settlement to cut me from his life. He was totally devastated and would never get over the shock of losing the most precious thing in his life. The more nasty it got between Richard and I the more smooth it became between Roger and Gail. It was very hard for me to cope with the constant disappearance of Roger to be with his wife, and she lived in a constant state of discomfort because of it. They still worked together and that meant they still socialised together to a degree and that was hard to bear. Roger couldn't seem to come to terms with letting her out of his life. What he really wanted was to have his cake and eat it. And don't they all. The months went by. Christmas was very difficult for all of us. Roger spent New Year's Eve at the dinner/dance in the hotel near where we met, and I was left on my own. He rolled in about 3am and I confronted him. I was disgusted with his behaviour and felt terribly let down. He said he had done it to keep the peace. I didn't feel at all peaceful! That didn't seem to matter.

It wasn't until the next round of events that things came to a head. At the start of April it would be Gail's fortieth birthday and their daughter Lori's thirteenth birthday, two major days to be dealt with. A few days before I had to sign my divorce papers and was feeling very sick at the thought of that. I came out of solicitors feeling vulnerable and was looking forward to a hug from Roger to make me feel better. I got home and the phone went. It was Roger. 'Oh good' I thought. He's rung to see how I am and make me smile. His voice sounded very strange though. He was faltering in what he was saying and it was nothing to do with me, but how sorry he was and he had been driving round for hours and hours and would have to come home and talk to me. I became very puzzled at his tone and awaited his arrival. What ensued made me physically sick. Roger announced he was going to leave me and go back to his wife! He could not bear to be away from her. He only loved me 50% and his wife and kids 50% and he should be with them. It took a while before it sunk in. What had I given up to be with him and now he was going. I became an emotional wreck, pleading with him not to go. I even thought I had changed his mind that evening, but the next day he said he was still determined to go. I refused to leave the house while he packed his bags and it was all so terribly painful I was actually sick. This particular period of time coincided with Easter when my children were going to their Dad's for four days. I was left completely on my own. I could not function. I could not eat or sleep, only drink and smoke to excess. My mind was numb. I just existed for those four days. This man had reduced me to something I would have frowned at in other people being so weak as to let a man take over their life like he had done. I had let myself love him wholly and completely and he had not loved me back, so he said. And worst of all I did not see it coming. He was so clever at hiding his feelings so as not to hurt, to both me and Gail, and I did not have any idea he could not cope with the situation. It was Easter Saturday. I got up and decided I needed a distraction or I was going to go mad. My girls had asked many times for a pet and I decided on a whim to buy a rabbit. I chose one, loaded up the hutch and rabbit in her car and arrived home with the new male in my life who would be reliable, a friend, be loving and loyal and not let me down. I staggered in the front door with hutch, rabbit food and bedding, to find a hand delivered letter laying on the mat. I recognised the type print Roger always used to use when he wrote those beautiful letters and started shaking. I put it on the side and refused to open it for a little while until I had psyched myself up for what it might say.

The relief was enormous. He said how wrong he was in the decision he made to go back. How he could not think of anything else but me and bitterly regretted his actions. He realised what it would mean to live life without me and couldn't bear to contemplate it and he would sort things out. I was full of emotional turmoil. Relief that he realised his love for me was too strong to ignore; anger, because he had put me through a most terrible ordeal, and confusion as to his mental instability. It seemed when he was with me he wanted his wife and when he was with his wife he wanted me. This was no basis for a future but I knew he was my future and I was his and he had obviously realised this now. The letter was swiftly followed by a phone call. There were tears and heartache. We loved each other and would be together again he said. I could only wait and see what happened. Roger had managed yet again to keep Gail and I dangling on a string. It took him three months to leave his wife a second time and again there was much trauma. Roger and I had arranged a holiday in Amsterdam for a week and that was to be the start of a new beginning for us. He returned to our rented house on 13 July of that year. He missed several social occasions he had promised me he would be at. He let me down constantly. I did indeed feel like his mistress. I wondered if I would ever be able to get on with my life again. Ever since I met this man he had caused me so much pain and heartache. However he did return with his belongings. We began to plan ahead. We decided it would be better, now that my divorce settlement was through, that we should buy a property rather than rent, so not being one to delay anything which I could attend to immediately, I set the wheels in motion. I soon found an ideal house in an ideal location and proceeded with the purchase. Roger went and viewed it with me and agreed it was just right. Three weeks later we jetted off on holiday.

It seemed to me that the holiday went so fast. We lived it up and had a great time. Or so I thought. We laughed and joked together, got drunk together, ate wonderful meals together and made the most passionate love together. It was time out for both of us, away from the pressures of home. Occasionally Roger would get a far-away look in his eyes and I would ask if everything was ok; he always said fine. Funny though, when we were at the airport, and were reviewing the holiday, I said what a great holiday it had been and he said it wasn't really a holiday merely a break. I thought at the time what an odd thing to say, however dismissed it, but it became crystal clear very soon afterwards.

It was exactly three days after the holiday. I had to sign the documents to buy the house I had found. My appointment wasn't until later that afternoon so I took my kids to the beach and had a lovely day in the sunshine. I met my sister and happily chatted about the great holiday, until it was time to go home and change to see my solicitor. I hurried home, dumped my bags in the kitchen and went upstairs. It was funny I didn't notice at first. It wasn't until I sat at the dressing table to put on some lipstick that I realised Roger's aftershave was missing. I stood up and opened the wardrobe door to find all his stuff was gone. I went into panic mode and dragged drawers open only to find they were empty. I stood there stunned. Not again I cried. I was reeling from the shock. I very soon realized I had to pull myself together and get to the solicitors. I would still go through with buying the house even though quite how I was going to manage financially I had no idea. I went into automatic pilot and could hear the solicitor talking to me but I heard nothing. I signed the papers and went back to the house to try and absorb what had happened. He must have gone there knowing I was out, so as there would not be another begging and pleading to stay. It was a cowardly thing to do. I immediately sought consolation from my family who came round like a shot to support me.

Weeks later and I am in a weird world trying to make sense of it all. I organized the house move which though I say so myself went surprisingly well. Who needs a man I thought to myself. I was delighted to be making a fresh start. I had a lot of fun making the house my own with my girls. It was the happiest house I ever lived in. I had to supplement my part time job with working in a pub in the evenings and cleaning jobs but I was doing it for myself and my girls. I even started dating again, albeit half-heartedly.

It was weeks later, when I had just got in from work, when my mobile bleeped. I checked the message and was very surprised to see it was from Roger! It simply said 'do you fancy a shag?' A million thoughts went racing through my mind. Well he thinks he can play games does he? Well I can do that too. The idea was very tempting, but only if I could keep the control. I rang him back and said "why not?" We arranged to meet at the old house where the rental contract had almost expired, so it was still sparsely furnished. We spent a night of drinking and lovemaking and for a short while it seemed like we had not been apart. But Roger made it clear he was still intent on getting back with his wife, so I decided that if I used him just for fun, no harm done. We started to meet secretly again and a few months went by. I was working at a local pub and he would ring me there and I would go over to his flat after work. My girls stayed at their dad's very regularly which freed me up. We began to see more and more of each other. I felt in control and let him do and be what he wanted. It wasn't until one evening in the pub I worked in, when his wife Gail came in with another man. I was so shocked and shook with nerves that I couldn't serve them and got another member of staff to do it! He was her daughter's boyfriends' dad. They seemed to be getting on very well! Later that evening, Roger rang me at the pub and I told him his wife had been in having a drink with this man. Roger was stunned. He then became euphoric. At last he had a get out of jail free card. He was off the hook. We could be together. His wife lied to him that she had been at home doing the ironing. She wasn't aware Roger and I were in touch.

Things began to fall into place after that, with Roger living in his flat, me at the house and weekends together. Within six months we knew we should buy a house together and we chose a beautiful converted barn where we spent five years, got married, and had a ball.

Fun, Fun, Fun

Our lives were running more and more smoothly and we began making the most of everything. This entailed much eating, drinking and a whirlwind of social events. Money was no problem and we lived well. Roger is a rugby fanatic and played for a local team for many, many years. The social side of rugby is full on, and I learned fast how to cope with keeping up with the boys in the bar after a game. Not many of the spouses and girlfriends seemed to be a part of that, but wherever Roger went, I went. It was what he wanted, and what I wanted. All the other guys seemed to like having me around too, so that's the way it was. We frequently went on coach trips to Twickenham, home of rugby, starting the day at 8am with a huge fry up in a local pub and a few large gin & tonics to wash it down. You can see how messy the day would get. But it was all good clean fun, everyone having a lovely time, lots of laughs and excitement watching England play. We had no concern for how all this fast food and constant flow of alcohol would affect our bodies, and for those with the constitution of an ox, it never seems to matter. I guess if you treat your body badly, the chances are that it will show up somewhere along the line. But for the time being, we were relatively young and hell bent on enjoying life to the full, and we did.

It was May 2001, my 45th birthday. Roger planned a night away in a beautiful small castle not too far from us. This castle had been converted into a high class restaurant, with bedroom suites with four poster bed and furniture befitting the period, all set in stunning manicured grounds in the countryside. When we arrived a valet parked Roger's car, a deep red TVR, polished and gleaming. I sometimes thought the car got more attention than me. We checked in, then had to wait in the library to be escorted up to our room. It was stunning, with mullion windows opening onto a pretty courtyard. We tucked straight into large gin & tonics which we had smuggled in, and soon it was time to get ready for dinner. It was at that point that Roger gave me my birthday present. It was a pair of sapphire and diamond drop earrings. They were exquisite. I put them on but felt they were obscured by my hair, which at the time was long dark curly tentrils. I realised I had nothing to put my hair up with . . . until Roger owned up that he might have something that would do. He produced a sex toy he was given as a joke that he had bought along to have some fun with. It was merely a black rubber ring, and perfect to hold my hair up. Laughing and sniggering, I wore it to dinner, where it was so refined dining, you could only hear the sounds of cutlery and glasses clinking, apart from us stifling laughter. I don't suppose anyone noticed my little secret, especially as the earrings were so beautiful! Roger and I were always looking for ways to have fun. Life was a breeze and we were carefree. We were usually busy planning the next event, whether it was with the rugby crowd or having fun dinner parties. I remember one dinner party we organised where we decided to have a Greek evening, and one couple arrived in togas and laurel wreaths which was highly entertaining as they were the only ones dressed up. At the time I was working for an auction house, and often there were lots which hadn't been sole on the monthly auction day, and sometimes these lots were sold afterwards at much reduced prices. I bought an old fashioned whole dinner service for £5, to use for our Greek night. We asked our dinner guests to take great care with the dinner service as it was a family heirloom. In fact it was pretty hideous but they were none the wiser. After the food was served and eaten, Roger stood up and said," You know I never liked these plates," and "I can't be bothered to wash them all up." With that he picked up his plate and threw it over the heads of everyone. It hit the wall, smashed and dropped into a basket we had placed there on purpose. The faces of our guests were a picture. The look of horror at what he had done soon changed into peals of laughter as we explained the joke, and they all proceeded to throw their own plates in the same way. We had little washing up to do that night!

We enjoyed a period of freedom and sun and thought it would never end.

The First Time

August 2006

*I*n August 2006 I was diagnosed with breast cancer. At this present point in time statistics tell us that one in nine women will get breast cancer, and if you look around at your family and friends, chances are at least one of them will have had cancer or will get it. That is a very disturbing thought. I am one of five children and from time to time in the past, in a morbid moment, have wondered who would be the first to have something life threatening and shake the foundations of our family unit. I have wondered how I would deal with the worry and concern for that family member, never thinking it might be me, but now somehow grateful that it is me, to save me the worry of constantly thinking about that person and what I could be doing to make things better for them. So this is my story, and it is told with the hope that if you have ever suffered from breast cancer, or do in the future, you will have read about someone similar to you, and it may give you comfort and hope for the future.

For anyone who has ever contracted this disease, they will all be able to tell you exactly when they first discovered it and how it affected them. For myself, this reared its ugly head in my 50th year. I really wasn't looking forward to being 50, as I had always hated any "0" birthday. It wasn't a call for a celebration in my book. Getting older and time passing should be mourned not celebrated. I actually spent the day with my four siblings and their partners. Eight of us went to my eldest sister's house. It was a particularly sunny day in May and we celebrated with champagne and strawberries on the train. We all trundled to a Chinese restaurant where you could eat as much as you liked for ten pounds. One of my sisters had obtained lots of pictures of me on various occasions when I was having a good time, usually glass in one hand and cigarette in the other, and she had laminated them and laid them down as place mats on the table. We all had a good laugh at them, and so did other onlookers at the restaurant! We had a great time and I forgot the reason why we were all together on that occasion.

My life is a busy one. I had been working full time up to that point, but was looking around for a part time job, so that I could develop my own business alongside. I had got back into making novelty cakes and was keen to progress that while I had a steady income to support me. I had my three lovely girls and a step daughter living at home, a wonderful husband and two dogs. All in all, a very normal life. Luckily I stumbled across a part time job, working as a PA/Office Manager in a local restaurant and cocktail bar. It suited me perfectly and I was delighted to be offered the job, so I handed in my resignation, and had to work a four week notice. It was within that four weeks that my life was about to be changed forever. One evening I was lying in bed, contemplating my change of job, one arm behind my head. I scratched an itch on that arm with my left hand, and in bringing my hand back, brushed it across my right breast. I felt something and touched it again to investigate. Yes there was definitely a lump there that I hadn't noticed before. Not that I was very vigilant about checking my breasts on a regular basis for lumps like we are all told to do. At the time, I dismissed it as regular hormonal lumpiness, and fell asleep. The next morning, in the shower I remembered about it and felt again. Yes it was still there but oddly, there seemed to be another lump near it. Well it was definitely normal hormonal lumpiness I thought, and got on with my day. Over the next few days I kept revisiting it in my mind and mentioned it to Roger. He smiled and with a cheeky look said "Well I hadn't noticed it before; I'm sure it's nothing, but maybe you should get it checked out." I was annoyed at the prospect of having to go to my G.P. and yet a nagging thought would not go away. One doctor's appointment later, she had said that due to my history of cysts (I'd had a massive ovarian cyst removed when I was 22—it weighed three quarters of a stone!), she was sure it was nothing but would refer me to the local hospital for a checkup. Now I was REALLY annoyed. I hadn't got time for all this fuss. The current NHS regulations state that every woman referred for breast lumps must be seen within two weeks of referral. My appointment came through exactly two weeks after my doctor's appointment and I realised I would have started my new job by then. Great! I felt guilty having to ask for time off as soon as I walked through the door! I toyed with the idea of not going, then conscience got the better of me and I thought about delaying the appointment, but Roger told me not to be ridiculous and go at the appointed time.

I told my new boss I had to go for a regular well woman's appointment and would be an hour or so late for work but would make it up at the end of the day. He was fine about it.

Hospital waiting rooms are depressing places to be aren't they? I didn't want my husband to come with me. I didn't see any need. It was busy. The seats were all full of people, and I sat there looking around wondering if it was like this every week. I was called into a room where there was a doctor and two nurses, one a trainee, I was informed. She examined my breasts and asked if I would mind the trainee doing the same. She then said she would try to extract fluid from the lumps and if they were cysts, fluid would come out and I could go home. Good. I could get off to work. They were running nearly an hour late at the hospital already and it was only 10 to 10 in the morning! How does that happen? She couldn't seem to get any fluid out but took samples of stuff onto slides. I didn't think anything of it, other than this was delaying me getting off to work. She said she would like me to go for a mammogram and gave me a piece of coloured paper with my details on it. I was sent off through a labyrinth of corridors to find the mammogram unit. On the way feeling a bit lost I stopped at a reception point to ask the way. Damn I knew her. She asked how I was and I said fine, but I would hardly have been asking for directions to the mammogram unit for fun would I? Well for any woman who has not had the dubious pleasure of a mammogram, let me tell you, I can't understand how breasts don't stay permanently flattened by this horrible machine. A nurse 'loads' your breast into a vice like press which then takes pictures of the inside. Very undignified! I went back to another waiting room, only to be called ten minutes later to have an ultrasound. Unaware that I needed an ultrasound,

I was guided into another room where there was a male doctor and a nurse waiting for me. More bemused and bewildered than anything else I disrobed again and told to lie on the bed. Having had ultrasounds before when I was expecting my children, this was nothing to fear apart from the cold gel they spread about first. Having done that, the doctor said he may as well do a biopsy as they will only ask for it later. Still I thought no more about it other than why would they want that and the fact that I was getting later and later for work. Well get on with it I thought and he did. He first of all injected my right breast about 10 times with anaesthetic. That felt weird. He then informed me I would only feel pushing but would hear the sound like a stapler would make. And the similarity in sound was accurate. He took two biopsies from each lump, stuck plasters on me, told me it would be sore for a few days and sent me back to the first doctor's waiting area. Some of the faces were the same as before. Eventually I was called back in and this time there were three other nurses in the room. The doctor began to explain that I had two 'very suspicious lumps' and I would have to wait for the biopsy results for it to be confirmed, which would take a week. A WEEK! What to be confirmed? The dawning of a very terrifying thought crossed my mind. She couldn't be talking about cancer, could she? I looked at her incredulously and asked her, did she mean cancer. She looked away from me to her screen and said very possibly. I said, can't you be more specific than that and she then said it was almost definitely cancer, but we would have to wait for the results. At that point the door opened and I was aware of several other hospital staff rushing in. Fear began rising in my throat and tears forced themselves upwards. The doctor looked at me mystified and asked me hadn't I thought it could be cancer? Everyone I had spoken to about this had reiterated my own thoughts, it was just cysts. A woman bent down to me and introduced herself as my new consultant who would be dealing with my case. WHAT CASE I wanted to scream. Another nurse said she was the Macmillan support nurse for me. This was all too much. I began to hyperventilate and someone asked if there was anyone I could contact? I was ushered into a side room, where I looked at the Macmillan nurse in total confusion and asked her do I have cancer? After hesitating she said yes. I reeled from the shock. She encouraged me to ring my husband, who unbeknown to me had come over to the hospital earlier and was waiting in the car park for me to emerge, all smiles. I merely asked him to meet me outside in a few minutes. The nurse hurriedly made me an appointment for the following Friday for the biopsy results, and herded me out of the building without passing all the other women waiting for their results, so that they would not see the rising fear in my eyes. I walked around the outside of the building in the drizzling rain trying to locate my husband in the sea of cars, frantically trying to think of a way of telling him. I stood in a lay-by and he drove over to meet me. I took a deep breath, climbed in and looked at him. That was one of my hardest moments. He crumbled with shock. We were both unable to stop the tears. We sat in stunned silence and tried to absorb the news. They must have got the results muddled up with someone else. I felt fine. There was nothing wrong with me. I was fine. I was in total denial at first, followed by a sinking feeling that this was really happening to me. I couldn't possibly go to work now I thought. I got my husband to ring them and merely say they were so slow at my check-up, it had got so late I wouldn't now be in today. The only people who knew I had

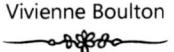
an appointment were one of my sisters, my best friend and my husband. What could I say?

A million thoughts go racing through your brain. I had a week of knowing I had cancer but not knowing anything about it. How advanced was it? How quickly was it growing? Had it spread? How long had I got? It was absolutely sick making. There is nothing I can say that would prepare anyone in that position for that week; suffice to say it was the longest week of my life. I couldn't believe it took a week to get those results. It was a week of sheer purgatory. I told my brother and sisters, and my best friend. I swore them to secrecy, until I had had the next appointment, when I would have much more information. My husband and I went and sat on the seafront together in stunned disbelief. It felt like someone had died. Why was everyone going about their day so normally? Didn't they know what was happening to me? It was sunny. Horrible things don't happen when it's sunny.

Quite how I got through that week I am not sure; what made matters worse was the lumps felt bigger. I just remember feeling very glad to be going to my next appointment and finding out exactly what was what, but also petrified and not wanting to go at all. Still, not going at all wasn't going to change what was wrong. This time my husband came with me. I was very grateful for his moral support. Again there were many women in the waiting area. I looked around and felt so sorry for them all. Some were just about to go through what I had gone through the previous week; some were probably at the same stage as me; some had had operations and chemotherapy and were there for the check-ups which follow on, probably scared half to death that the cancer might have come back. What a depressing scene.

We were ushered into a room where the consultant was waiting along with two other nurses. I have to say she was extremely good in the way she approached me with the news. Her bedside manner was fantastic. She explained everything in a very practical and positive manner, and her body language was very reassuring. She sat very close to me with her leg touching mine and told me I had two tumours each approximately 2.5cms long in my right breast. This categorised them as Grade 2 tumours, Grade 1 being not so worrying and Grades 3 and 4 being pretty serious. They were cancerous and I had probably had them for up to eighteen months! They were slow growing and therefore not life threatening at that point, but I would be facing surgery within a month. She also explained the lumps would have felt bigger due to the biopsies. I really wished someone had told me that at the time to save me further worry. As the lumps were in the same breast and of the size they were I was told I would have to have a mastectomy. This was all new territory for me. I still couldn't believe she was talking about me! Also, because of the possibility that the cancer had spread, I would have to have all the lymph nodes removed from under my arm, as this is where it spreads to next, and also remove the nipple as that would probably be infected too. There were several ways they could reconstruct the breast if I so wished. The first was to remove fat from the stomach and replace the breast tissue with that, but she decided that wouldn't be an option for me as I wasn't carrying enough fat—small comfort! The second was to remove muscle from one's back and add an implant.—a very invasive surgery I couldn't contemplate. The third was to insert a tissue expander under the muscle and inflate it with a saline solution gradually to create a new breast shape, and several months later, remove the tissue expander and put an implant in place. At that point they could create a new nipple and tattoo around it to make it look realistic. They could also nip and tuck the other breast to realign them. Well I certainly hadn't expected to get a "boob job" but it seemed that this last option was going to be the one for me, if it really was me they were talking about. It all seemed very unreal. I was very glad to have my husband there as another pair of ears, to try and take all the information in, and I would advise anyone who was faced with that consultation to have someone with you.

Down to practicalities, the National Health Service could offer me this operation in about two months, due to current waiting lists and the length of the operation, it would be performed in a hospital 25 miles away. It seemed a very long time to wait to me. I was very lucky in that my husband had subscribed to BUPA for a number of years due to being self-employed and had also put me and our children on it too. I was quite happy to be with the NHS but if BUPA could do it quicker then that was what I would do. The NHS consultant was extremely helpful and agreed I should find out if this was possible. She recommended a consultant she knew, who also did private work. He was a plastic surgeon by profession and she gave me his number.

That weekend I had arranged to go out to dinner with my best friends. I really wanted to go and they promised to just be 'normal' and not speak about it at all or I would cry and I didn't want my mascara to run. They were so good and didn't mention it at all. We sat round the table in the restaurant and they were laughing and joking with my husband, and I looked at them all and felt so very, very sad. A little voice in my head kept saying "You've got cancer don't forget. Life will never be the same again." It was hard for me to behave in my normal carefree way.

I went to see the consultant the following week and he did a full diagnosis, confirming everything the NHS had told me. This second opinion made me realise this was no mistake. It was really happening to me and I was facing surgery and chemotherapy within two weeks. He began to explain what the surgery would involve, and showed me a tissue expander and an implant. He also told me he would have to remove the lymph nodes from under my arm, as this was an area that the cancer could have travelled to. At this point in time there wasn't a machine to detect cancer in the lymph nodes, so surgeons had to take this precautionary measure. (Since I had my operation lots of people did a charity midnight walk to raise funds in my area to buy such a machine. They did raise enough money and it will make a big difference in the future for some women who will now not have to endure that part of an operation unnecessarily). I signed the paperwork allowing this operation to proceed—like I had a choice, and he explained all the things that could go wrong during and after the operation. How bizarre it all was! I found myself nodding and smiling and making jokes about it all. Well it could hardly be taken seriously because it wasn't me he was talking about . . . he said while I was there I should have a liver, stomach and lung Xray and ultrasound to be sure the cancer hadn't spread further. Yet more stress while I waited for those results which were immediate. They were clear! I was full of smiles for a few minutes, so relieved I only had to face the breast surgery. When life throws even worse possibilities at you, it makes the original problem see less huge.

Now for the really hard bit. I had to face telling my children. My eldest daughter had been working in America and flew back on the Sunday before I was due to go into hospital. I decided not to tell her till she was at home. Every time I had to tell someone about it, I started to shake and my voice sounded strange. I could only take shallow breaths and speak in short sentences. We all cried and held hands, but I tried my hardest to sound positive and that it was not a big deal. One thing I did not want, was for the news to spread too far, or indeed for the facts to be distorted like Chinese Whispers. Gradually I informed family and close friends, and left it at that, but I was not prepared when I bumped into people I hardly knew, for them to come up to me and say how sorry they were to hear my news and how was I! I was just beginning to realise how fast bad news travels. I didn't like it one little bit, being the centre of attention for this reason. It was all absolutely horrible and I wanted it all to go away. I had to tell my new boss about the situation of course and felt terrible as I had only been working for him for 4 days when I first found out about all of this. Timing was of course bad as he had taken some much earned leave as soon as he had me in place to cover the office. He was on holiday in Milan and I had no choice but to tell him then as my first operation was imminent. He was so lovely about it and put my mind at ease saying not to worry, it was unforeseen circumstances and he would support me all he could. It made me even more determined not to let him down and to carry on as normally as possible.

The day of the pre-operation appointment came. Roger took me over to the hospital and waited with me while I had blood tests and heart monitoring to check I was fit and well enough to have the operation. There was lots of form filling and introductions to various hospital staff who would be looking after me. I went about it all in rather a daze just accepting what was coming with resignation. There was absolutely no choice about this. I had to go through with it no matter how I felt about it all.

Friday 15th September 2006 arrived as of course was inevitable. My bag was packed and I said goodbye to my children. I was very tearful but trying desperately to put on a brave face. I told them if they wanted to visit that would be lovely but if they didn't feel they could that was totally understandable. I remember going to visit my own mother when I was a teenager, after she'd had a stomach operation. It was my first visit to a relative in hospital and I was shocked and frightened to see all of the tubes going into her and all of the machines surrounding her. Those images are imprinted in my memory. It is a harsh reality to see someone you love in that situation.

We arrived at the hospital which would be my world for the next week. I was put into a private room and throughout the next few hours had a succession of nurses doing things to me in readiness. One very touching moment was when a knock on the door revealed the delivery of the most beautiful bouquet of flowers from Roger which instantly made me cry. My consultant came in, in his operating greens, which was disconcerting, and drew diagrams all over my chest in felt pen. How odd to be standing in front of a stranger who was drawing all over me. He informed me he had a procedure (that's what they call operations these days) to perform on a lady before me whose operation was not as complicated as mine, so I had another couple of hours to wait. The anaesthetist came in and had a chat about what type of aesthetic I would like. Like? None actually. And how could I possibly make a choice? I rather left it up to him, with the proviso that I didn't want anything spinal, and that I did not want to wake up with an oxygen mask over my face or I would panic! I also had a sickness reaction to anaesthetic so he promised lots of anti-sick drugs. He was a quietly spoken gentle man with an excellent bedside manner which helped a lot. He told me not to worry and he would look after me throughout the operation. At least that was reassuring.

Roger stayed with me until I was given a pre-med to relax me. He then slipped away before they came for me. That parting was very hard and it makes me tearful now to think of it. By now it was about 4pm and I was anxious to get it over with. A nurse came in and escorted me to the operating theatre. That was weird taking myself to the theatre. I felt like a lamb to the slaughter. I was grateful that I wore contact lenses and had to remove them before theatre, so I couldn't actually see very clearly. Having said that, it was all too clear to me when I was led into the room where there were lots of bright lights over a very narrow operating table and was told to climb onto it. Nursing staff and the anaesthetist were busying themselves around me chatting and it felt surreal. I thought 'I could get off this and run away at high speed and I would be fine, but of course I wouldn't be fine, so I lay there shaking uncontrollably and then my lights went out.

I awoke five hours later in recovery. I was aware of people talking around me, a conversation about buying a house. As I started to come to, I began shaking huge shivers. One man said 'you are okay, lots of people have this reaction to the anaesthetic and I was given another shot of something. After half an hour I was wheeled back to my room. It wouldn't have surprised me if they had made me walk that bit too! Roger was waiting in my room. Great relief it was over flooded through me and I began to feel elated, and hungry. I demanded bacon sandwiches and cups of tea. I felt remarkably good. For the next six hours Roger and I talked and talked; I cannot remember what about now. He was advised at about 3am the next morning it would be a good idea to go home and get some rest. And I slept.

My consultant informed me that the cancer had spread to one of the lymph nodes but he had removed all of those that might had been affected too under my arm. (I think 14 in all) his additional surgery meant my right arm movement was severely restricted. It all felt very numb. He told me he had put some saline solution into the tissue expander to start it off and would add more solution periodically over the next few weeks until it was fully inflated. He gave me a funny looking gadget which I had to bring with me each time, which located the point in the tissue expander where he must inject.

My hospital stay lasted 6 days in all. The days passed slowly. The weather outside was warm and sunny for mid-September, and gradually I shuffled outside into the grounds for fresh air, with my three chest drains attractively dangling at my side. Someone bought me a present in a flowery gift bag, so I popped the drains into it when I was wandering around. That looked much better! On the third day one of the drains was removed but I was told I could not go home until there was less than 40milograms of fluid in the other two bags. I knew I had to face looking at myself in the mirror and was petrified at what I would see. I couldn't bring myself to look so I didn't. I had a select number of visitors, my family and two friends. I had stipulated that I did not want any men to visit me at all, except my brother; it wasn't like I had a broken leg; it was a very personal issue and I was particularly sensitive about that. I had many texts and cards from well-wishers. My new boss even rang the hospital to see how I was and they put him through to me for a chat. He was so kind. Roger stayed with me practically all the time I was in hospital. He was my rock and I am forever grateful to him. It makes me tearful just to write this. I am not normally an emotional person, but this has overtaken me.

I couldn't wait to get home. It was touch and go whether they took the remaining two chest drains out or sent me home with them in. I really did not relish the thought of that, but they said they would remove them, but if the remaining fluid built up and it was swollen and painful I should go back to have it drained. What a disgusting thought. I was discharged from hospital with a variety of pills and some breast pads to pad out my bra while the new breast was being created, and sent home. How wonderful that felt. To have a shower and be in my own bed, without the noise of beepers going off at all times of the day and night.

Having said that, when you first get home there is a feeling of vulnerability without a nurse at your beck and call. Over the next week there was a build-up of fluid but I managed to wait until my post-operative check-up to have a needle stuck into it to drain it. The anti-sickness drugs stop you being sick but they also stop natural bodily functions, which made me feel horrible. The whole area of the operation from the middle of my breast plate round to my back on the right side was numb. As time went on I began to wonder just how much feeling was going to come back. I was given exercises to do to get full mobility back into my arm. They were hard work and painful, as the tendons under my arm had to be stretched. I was warned to try and get my arm back to normal quickly as this helped in the fight against something called lymphedema which is essentially the arm swelling up with fluid. Sometimes this happens and it stays like it. I had decided that wasn't going to happen to me. (Like you get a choice in how your body reacts to things!) In fact I had decided I would have none of the possible negative results of an operation such as mine. This cancer was a major inconvenience to me but I was damned if I was going to be inconvenienced by anything else!

Well the time came when I had to remove the dressings which had protected me from seeing the full extent of the wound. I had tried to mentally prepare myself for this. I knew it wasn't going to be pretty. I had always tried to take care of my body and prided myself on a generally good physique for a 50 year old. Being a rather vain person this mutilation was a huge blow to me. I wasn't sure how I was going to come back from it mentally. I stood in the shower and peeled the big plaster off without looking underneath. So far so good. Then, after my shower I stood in front of the sink to clean my teeth and looked in the mirror without thinking. Oh my God what have they done to me? There was a mound of skin stretched tightly over a hard lump with one scar running horizontally from just right of my breast plate to under my arm. It looked so weird with no nipple. Well there could be no more shocks I thought. And this was temporary I kept reminding myself. Some women do not opt for a reconstruction. They just (she says as if it's an insignificant thing) have a mastectomy and are completely flat on one side—or both sides if they are unlucky enough to have a double mastectomy. In recent years reconstructions have developed significantly and 'before' and 'after' pictures reveal just how successful it can be. More and more women who have had a mastectomy years ago are now opting for a reconstruction, which actually was an option for me to leave it for a while, but I felt I might as well go for the whole works at once. Over time I became accustomed to how I looked but I could not bring myself to show Roger. It was such a difficult place to be in my head. We had only been married four years and he adored my body. What on earth was he going to think now? I just could not show him.

I knew the next trauma I would have to face was the chemotherapy. I was given advice of what to expect and none it sounded very appealing! What worried me was the possibility of losing my hair. Being rather vain I was fretting about outward appearances. I rushed into town and bought false eyelashes and eyebrow pencil, and found a shop locally which sold soft turban style caps so I bought a couple of those, just in case. I didn't want to be caught out. A friend who had had chemotherapy and lost all of her hair told me of a place about 30 miles away which supplied wigs for hair loss. I decided I would buy a wig just in case and have peace of mind rather than leave it until my hair did fall out and then have to go out and find one. My husband came with me to help choose the wig, and we had quite a fun afternoon. The man who was attending to me was rather gorgeous which helped! At the time my own hair was shoulder length and cut into a messy bob. It was naturally curly and coloured to death to cover the ever increasing amount of grey! I chose a short spiky style, the same colour as my own as I hoped if I did have to wear it, people would think I had just had my own hair cut. No one need know about me. Roger said it looked fantastic and I should have my own hair styled like the wig! I felt better about it all and most of all prepared.

Two weeks later I started my course of chemotherapy. This phase of my treatment was to rather take over my way of life. I was told I should have six courses three weeks apart, which was the 'normal' amount of chemotherapy given to women in my situation. After an initial assessment of fitness, blood condition etc. I was certified ready to go. The whole procedure took about four hours. Once they had taken blood, it was analysed and a specific formula of drugs was made up. I was advised that I could wear a cold cap to help prevent hair loss. This is a very unattractive hat rather like a jockey's hat which had been chilled to—5° and strapped on, changed every half an hour. It is put on half an hour before the chemotherapy drugs are administered and kept on for half an hour afterwards. This works for some people I was told. Well I would certainly give it a go if it meant I kept my hair. Hair loss is such a difficult thing to come to terms with as it affects how you feel about yourself. Additionally you then obviously look ill to everyone else. The fewer people who knew about it all, the better it suited me. The cold cap was indeed cold, but bizarrely in a bearable sort of way. Maybe it was my hope that it may do a good job of keeping my hair on my head. The thought of it now makes me feel sick. I was warned that I may suffer from association sickness and over the course of the next few months was to learn that yes I did get quite a lot of that. The nurse fitted a cannula into a vein in my hand, which is a long needle with attachments for a drip and access to the vein to put the drugs into my body. Some people don't have very prominent veins and after a couple of treatments have to have a Pic line permanently attached into a vein in their arm. I sincerely hoped I wouldn't need to have that unsightly thing done to me. As it turned out I got away with not having a Pic line fitted. The nurse told me I had 'cracking' veins, as in 'good', but that didn't stop the very painful after-effects from the damage the drugs do to the veins, each time I had a chemotherapy treatment. The nurse set up a saline drip to flush the veins through and then the drugs arrived on the ward. She sat by me in the hospital bed and proceeded firstly to give me an anti-sickness injection and a steroid injection. Then she began to inject five large syringes of drugs into me. I was on a course called FEC chemotherapy. Two of the syringes were bright red and I was informed this would turn my pee red for a day or so. Lovely! It took about three quarters of an hour. It did make the vein very painful and stung a bit but I coped. She then put up another saline bag to flush the drugs through. When she took the last cold cap off there were ice crystals on my hair! This was the pattern of each chemotherapy session. I was given my next treatment date, a phone number to ring if I needed it, lots of pills for anti-sickness, steroids, and antibiotics, and allowed to go home.

Over the next few hours I thought I had got away without any horrible side effects. I was ravenous and we bought huge portions of fish and chips which was lovely. It wasn't until the following day that I began to feel absolutely shattered. I am normally a very active person, rarely ill and intolerant of people who wallow in their beds. But I had no choice. Day one was exhausting! There are quite a number of side-effects which chemotherapy can cause. Some women don't get any, some have a few and some have a lot of problems because of it, and the side-effects can change with each chemotherapy session. For myself, I did get some, but on the whole coped reasonably well in spite of it. I can only compare the sickness side of it with morning sickness. Feeling sick is one of the worst in my book. You can't get away from it. That feeling did go away after a few days with the help of the pills. The tiredness also got better after a few days but increasingly worse with each treatment. The steroids upset my digestive system but that too subsided after a while As a result of the steroids I put on half a stone in weight over the whole course of treatment which I was really fed up with. I stamped around the house moaning that a lot of people lost weight with cancer and here I was getting fatter! I did get indigestion quite a bit throughout all the chemotherapy but it shouldn't have been a surprise to me, stuffing my face with food all the time! I had days when I just could not stop eating! I felt near to exploding but still I would cram it into my mouth. As a person who was careful to maintain a healthy weight normally, this insatiable appetite was proving hard to control . . . Unfortunately the food which I ate immediately following a chemotherapy session, I later had an aversion to because of the association that particular food had with feeling sick. I tried to eat things I wasn't particularly fond of so it wouldn't matter if I went off it but it didn't really work like that. Nothing tasted right; I craved really salty or really sweet things in an attempt to find something that tasted like it should. One woman I knew of ate chicken salad every time she went to the hospital and ten years later still could not face chicken salad! I haven't had fish and chips since! I even grew to associate the roads we took to the hospital with feeling sick and any thoughts about the hospital or its staff caused nausea instantly.

It was two and a half weeks after my first chemotherapy. I was feeling reasonably pleased with myself as to how I had coped with things and prayed I could get through the next five sessions in a similar way. I made a pact with myself. For every horrible thing that was done to me, I could treat myself to something nice! By the time all of the chemotherapy was done I had a whole new wardrobe of clothes, shoes and handbags! It was a great idea! There's nothing like retail therapy for that feel-good factor, for me anyway. Roger and I were invited to a fund-raising day at the races to support Motor Neurone Disease. A very good friend of ours had died recently from this most horrible disease and we were eager to support his widow and have a lovely day out at the same time. I was standing in the shower that morning planning what to wear while I washed my hair. I plonked lots of conditioner on it and mused over the day to come. As I ran my fingers through my hair to spread the conditioner, I pulled my hand away to reveal thick strands of my hair stuck between my fingers. I looked at it in shock. Panic rising I shook it all off my hand and ran my fingers through my hair again. Exactly the same thing happened. My hair was falling out fast. I was devastated. Crying, I ran to Roger who tried comforting me. I had decided this was not going to happen to me, as though I could influence what side-effects I did and didn't get, but it was happening to me. I toyed with the idea of not going out for the day but would not let myself give in, so we went. But I was very conscious of hairs drifting onto my clothes and felt rather depressed. Over the next few days my hair thinned terribly. I lost all body hair apart from my eyebrows and eyelashes at that point. My self-confidence began to ebb away. I was going to have to resort to the wig.

Apart from having just over two weeks off work when I had the first operation, I had very little time off throughout the chemotherapy period. It was sometimes hard to drag myself to the office but it did wonders for a sense of normality. This was the best therapy I could have. Even if I had to come home and go straight to bed I would rather do that than stop working. I felt if I cut ties with the outside world it would be all the more difficult to get back into it afterwards. So that Monday morning I put on the wig and braved going to work. I felt hugely self-conscious at first, but every single person I met after that told me how fantastic my hair looked since I'd had it cut! I didn't let on it wasn't my own hair and gradually as the weeks went by I became used to wearing the wig when I was out and about. I ripped it off my head as soon as I got home though. It felt like a hat, and I was pleased that at least it was winter time this was all happening. I should imagine it could become quite unbearably hot to wear a wig in the summer months.

Each chemotherapy session brought additional symptoms with it. Everyone is different and so it affects people in different ways. But for me I suppose looking back I got off quite lightly. What I found very disconcerting was the fact that once chemo was under way and I met people I knew, they couldn't wait to tell me about so and so who they knew who only had two sessions and then got some horrible reaction and ended up in hospital on death's door, or their friend whose mouth was totally ulcerated and bled a lot, their sister's nails all went black, or their neighbour whose cancer came back twice more and had chemo three times but she's still here, as though that would make me feel better! If people would only stop and think before they blurted out tales of woe, about how that information would be received and how it would play on the recipient's mind in the middle of the night. I am quite a strong person but even so I had phases of self-doubt and depression about it all and that did not help at all. Did they really think it was going to cheer me up in any way? Only positive news is worth hearing; all else please keep to yourselves.

Generally the symptoms of chemotherapy are cumulative. If you feel tired after the first one you sure as hell are going to feel more tired after the sixth one. The tiredness is a strange sort of tiredness because it doesn't go away. You don't feel refreshed after a sleep. I could be in the middle of cooking dinner and suddenly feel shattered. I learned to have a rest in the afternoon sometimes, a very hard thing for me to make myself do. It seemed like giving in. One of my worst symptoms was the hot and cold sweats. Within a few hours of having the drugs injected it would begin. Within seconds my body would be running with sweat and I would take layers of clothes off. After about a minute I would go freezing cold and shivering and be putting three tops on and covering myself in a blanket to get warm. This happened about every ten minutes for days! It gradually dissipated but the nights were horrendous with lack of sleep and being drenched in sweat then not able to get warm. It was totally miserable. The oncologist said he didn't know if it was just my reaction to the chemotherapy or it was the fast onset of the menopause brought on by the chemotherapy and the symptoms of menopause at their most extreme. Little comfort for me!

I had other symptoms to a milder degree. My hairless skin felt glassy. That's the only way I can describe it. Moisturiser just slid over the surface. Most odd! I was given antibiotics to take every second week of chemotherapy. The idea behind this is preventative. Apparently people cope much better with infections which, in the second week, you are more susceptible to due to the immune system being at

its lowest. Of course that brought its own set of bodily reactions too, for example thrush. It is one of those unfair things in life that we are given drugs to help one condition and they cause another!

In the fourth week of each month when I was the best I could be, I revisited the hospital to have some more saline injected into the tissue expander. My consultant used the odd shaped magnet to locate where he must inject into the expander. He filled it with more fluid until I said it felt really tight, and the muscle and skin over the top were stretched until it felt like it would burst open. This feeling lasted a couple of days until the muscle gave way a little more. Gradually over the course of a few months and several injections it had stretched to a 36B to match my left breast. How clever is that!

Well I got through it all and rejoiced after the sixth and final chemo session. Gradually my body began to repair the damage. My hair started to come back. I never thought how pleased I would be to have to pluck my eyebrows (which I did mostly lose after the fourth chemo, along with my eyelashes) and shave my legs! I joined a gym to try and regain control of my weight. I was just starting to appreciate the thought of not having to trail back to the hospital when I received the paperwork telling me my admission date for the next reconstruction operation! Well I knew it was coming and I couldn't stay as I was with a tissue expander inside me. Whilst I had become accustomed to it, it felt like a boulder to touch and certainly looked very strange in the flesh, although I was the only one looking! I was given a date seven weeks after the last chemo. This was just about enough time for my body to fully repair itself.

By March I was ready to face the next operation. I was allocated a four day stay in hospital when the surgeon would remove the tissue expander and replace it with an implant, as you would have if you were opting for breast enlargement. I was also going to have the other breast lifted, (or nip and tuck) to realign the breasts. This was a much less daunting procedure than the first operation and I just wanted to get it over with. It meant having chest drains again which I was not best pleased to discover, and again it was explained to me all of the things that could go wrong, including implant rejection, intense bleeding and infection. I went into the operating theatre feeling very apprehensive but resigned. It was a Friday evening. The operation took two and a half hours. The surgeon was able to go in through the scar I had originally which was about 7 inches long, and insert the implant. This would mean less scarring eventually. The left breast was cut vertically downward from the nipple to the base and along the base in an anchor like shape. The nipple is actually removed and replaced higher up, therefore the nipple is sewn back on around the edge of the areola. I think this was more traumatic than the replacement of the implant.

During this hospital stay, I did not receive the same amount of care and attention as before. I tried on several occasions to call a nurse, and it was 15 minutes before anyone came. The nurse explained that they were very short staffed and she was the only regular member of staff on that night, and she had an orderly from a temping agency to help her, who didn't speak much English and didn't have any medical experience! Roger was with me at the time, but I would have felt very worried if I had been on my own, having just come out of surgery. I was so determined not to stay in hospital a minute longer than I had to and was delighted the following morning to be told I could go home. I had however to go home with chest drains in for a few days. They told me once there was less than a certain amount of fluid in the drain bags I could go back and have them removed. I was getting myself organised to go home, and went to put the alarm button on a lead by the bed back into its holder but it went straight through the holder and fell onto the floor. I picked it up and noticed it had fallen on the alarm button and activated a call for a nurse. I didn't need a nurse so I went over to the wall where there were two buttons, one of which I had seen the nurses press when they were answering a call to deactivate it. So I pressed the first button but I could still see the light outside my room flashing for attention and hear the beeper still going. So I pressed the other button and that didn't do any good either. Oh well I thought and carried on packing my bag. Suddenly my door burst open and seven staff came racing in with looks of emergency on their faces, shouting where's the patient? I realised I must have pressed the emergency button and the crash team had all arrived to help me. So there were in fact more staff around the hospital; they were all walking away muttering that they had to abandon other patients to attend to me! I said that perhaps if the alarm holder had been fixed it wouldn't have happened. I was glad to go home, with the chest drains in a plastic carrier bag

By the fifth day at home I had decided that the chest drains were coming out; I had had enough of carrying them around in a shoulder bag and changing the bags every day. So I left it rather later in the day to change the bags so there wouldn't be much fluid in them when I got to the hospital. They were satisfied and removed the bags. I knew this was not very clever as the fluid would only build up inside but I knew that would go in time. I am not good with pipes and tubes coming out of bodies! I did continue to recover well and returned to work and normal life quickly. I was told I would have to leave things to settle down before the last stage of having a nipple creation. I have since discovered that some women can have the nipple preserved if it is not infected, to be reused at this point. They have it grafted onto another part of their body for example their thigh until the time comes to graft it back in place! What a shocking thought. It is a brave woman who decides she can face having her nipple on her thigh for a while! I suppose if it means you end up with breasts that look identical, you could consider coping with that. However I had no choice which in some respects I am quite glad about!

I made a decision that by my birthday at the end of May, my hair might be good enough to abandon the wig and be natural again. I planned a big party at my home and invited 80 guests to share my celebrations of wellbeing. It marked a time when I felt I was moving on from all of the trauma of the last nine months. Hair that is growing back after chemotherapy is a bit strange. It is called chemo hair because it isn't like normal hair, rather like baby hair all wispy and crinkly and thin. I had been told that sometimes the hair grows back straight where it was curly before and vice versa, blonde where it was dark and dark where it was blond! I was really hoping my hair would grow back straight and black but it didn't. It grew back faded and more curly than before. I was bitterly disappointed! One of my daughters being a trained hairdresser, managed to reshape it a bit and coloured it to my natural dark brown, and with lots of styling cream I looked not too bad. All of my friends were so complementary (although I felt more out of kindness than honesty). What did surprise me was the reaction I got from other people not so close to me who hadn't known I had breast cancer. They were taken aback at the close cropped hair style I had but were all very flattering about it. This boosted my confidence greatly and I packed the wig away, hopefully never to wear it again! My eyelashes and eyebrows came back thicker and darker than before, and I can honestly say I benefitted from it all!

The coming out party took shape. I was still in recovery from chemotherapy so before the party, I laid down for a rest. Roger came in and sat on the bed beside me, offering me a cup of tea. Suddenly, he crashed to the floor, rolling around in pain. His knee had 'popped' again. This happened from time to time, and he would stretch it out and it would go back in. Well this time it didn't. We decided to get help, so rang my sister Christina, a physiotherapist, who came racing round. She tried and tried and couldn't get it back in. It was no good, he would have to have an ambulance. The paramedics eventually strapped him to a trolley and loaded him into the ambulance. My middle daughter arrived home and, seeing the ambulance outside, was freaked out thinking it was me. As he was carted off to hospital, the D.J. was arriving to set up! The food was arriving too, and it was chaos. I cried. This couldn't be happening to me. I wasn't even ready yet. Soon enough guests started arriving for the party, asking where Roger was. I explained briefly, praying he would be back soon, and enlisted help with drinks for everyone. The house filed up with guests, and eventually, the front door opened and there was Roger on crutches, drugged up with painkillers till he could have an operation in a couple of days' time. He arrived and everyone cheered and I was taken aback. It wasn't about him, this was my party. I leapt in front of him, and shouted "it's not about him, it's about me!" Everyone fell about laughing, and we settled him down in a corner, where he was a captive audience to anyone who cared to talk to him. He was not very amused! I, in the meantime had great fun, dancing with all the boys, while Roger could only sit and watch. I had a great time at my party. It was a huge success, and will stay in my mind as one of the few highlights of a very traumatic year. Roger had his knee operation and recovered well.

June saw me off once again to the consultant to discuss the nipple reconstruction. This was a real eye opener! He informed me that there were several ways of doing this. I could have a mould taken of the existing nipple and have a plastic one made to stick on! No thanks!! I could have a graft from another part of my body from somewhere where the skin was similar to that of a nipple. He suggested either the ear lobe (odd and not to my mind worth considering altering my pierced ears), or the labia! Well I was not about to let him go rummaging around down there! He said "By the look on your face that's not an option!" The last alternative which I decided I would go for, was to have "a bit of origami" as the surgeon put it, done on the skin, where it is gathered up and formed into a nipple. This method sounded the least invasive and would be a five minute job under local anaesthetic. Or so I thought. I signed the paperwork while he explained all the things that could go wrong, which is something they are legally obliged to do. Well if that doesn't put you off the idea nothing will! An appointment was made for the following month and it wasn't until a couple of days before the appointment that I began to question whether I really wanted to do this. Well I hadn't gone through all this reconstruction treatment to opt out at the last hurdle, so arrived at the hospital in an optimistic mood.

I was allocated a room, the look of which was beginning to become very familiar to me. I had the usual visits from nurses for blood pressure and temperature, and to answer a million questions I had been asked a million times before. I still could not believe they asked me my full name and date of birth! My ever attentive husband was with me, and we rolled our eyes at each other. It felt almost as if I was an imposter. Exactly who would go into a hospital to have a nipple reconstruction when they had two perfectly good nipples anyway was completely beyond me!

Things began to turn a bit more serious when the staff began treating the procedure like a proper operation. I thought it all seemed a bit over the top for "a bit of origami," but was not fazed by all the prep work going on. Then the nurse came to take me up to the theatre, and Roger asked how long I would be. The nurse said it would take about an hour. AN HOUR! What on earth was he going to do for all of that time? I suddenly began to realise there was going to be a bit more to this that I had thought. The walk to theatre was also becoming familiar to me; the bright lights and staff moving around with masks on. My surgeon was ready and waiting for me. I sat on the operating table while he drew lines on my breast so the alignment would be good. Then I was asked to lie down and he injected three times into my breast with a local anaesthetic. I was told it would sting but it didn't, probably because I have very little or no feeling in that breast or under my arm. I was right to feel apprehensive when I heard the word "scalpel please". I hadn't realised there was to be cutting and stitching. If I had really thought about it, of course there would have to be, as gathering skin and tying a knot in it would hardly had produced the desired result! I held the nurse's eye contact for 55 minutes while the surgeon cut, tugged, stitched and snipped, and was very relieved when he said "all done" and I was taken out on the trolley; not that I couldn't walk but Health and Safety regulations state we have to go back to the ward on a trolley. I was wheeled down the corridor and suddenly realised they were taking me into the post-operative recovery room. It was completely full of people still under general anaesthetic, with oxygen masks on, and various pipes and tubes coming out of them, with staff talking in low tones monitoring them all. I knew I really did not want to be there, and felt like a fraud. I asked the nurse if I could be moved out onto the corridor to wait for the ward nurse to fetch me, which she did and I was duly collected and returned to my room.

There is a lack of communication I have noticed, between staff at the hospital I stayed in, and I don't know if that is symptomatic of every hospital, private or NHS. After about half an hour a nurse came in and I said I would like a cup of tea, but he said I should start on water to see if I was sick. I explained I had not had a general anaesthetic and would be fine to drink and eat normally. Eventually I did get some sandwiches and became frustrated at being made to wait around, considering I was able to leave. I waited around for a while and then said to Roger "Well I am going home now." The nurse chased me down the corridor with the discharge paperwork with a smile on her face, saying, you are obviously ready to leave! Another Friday evening spent at the hospital. This was becoming a habit I was looking forward to breaking!

A week passed and I returned to see my consultant, for him to take the plaster off and check how I was doing. He seemed pleased with the results and said I should return in the Autumn for the final bit: the tattooing. The nurse got a mirror to show me how it looked and although the nipple looked rather 'button' like, he had done a brilliant job!

I was gradually being put back together.

The next landmark for me was a mammogram on the left breast (the good one) to see if it had spread. It had been a year since the first diagnosis. I actually approached this appointment with calmness and was not worrying that it could quite possibly be bad news. I felt fine, I looked well—but then I had felt fine and looked well before. Off we went again down on that familiar journey to the hospital. We were shown to a waiting room where Roger got out his trusty crossword book which had helped him while away the hours he had waited for me, and I was then shown to a changing room to put on the 'do up at the back' gown and dressing gown. The nurse said that I would have the Xrays done and the doctor would take a look at them while I was there and then I could go home! As said before, it's a wonder breasts ever recover their normal shape after a mammogram! As the nurse clamped my breast into the machine I shouted "Jesus!" it was quite painful! She showed me to another waiting area next to the Xray redevelopment room. She was chatting in a very light-hearted manner to another nurse and then their voices became low. I could not hear exactly what they were saying. An anaesthetist wandered past me into the room and I heard one of the nurses saying "oh let's ask him while he's here." The door was then shut. For the first time I began to feel sick. Something was wrong. Why had they shut the door? What had they seen on my X-rays? The door opened and the anaesthetist left saying "see what the doctor makes of it," and as he walked away the doctor passed me and went into the room. He shut the door. By this time a million thoughts were racing through my mind. I was back where I was a year ago, and I was going to have to go through it all again, but this time I knew what to expect and felt positively sick. Roger was only a corridor away from me and I had the same thoughts as before: how on earth am I going to tell him. The door opened again and one of the nurses came over to me and asked me to follow her into another room. She asked me to take the dressing gown off again and lay on the examination bed. I was very scared. The doctor came in and explained that there was a patch of dense tissue in the left breast that he would like to examine further with an ultrasound. It was very quiet in that room; I hardly dared breathe. He did the ultrasound and said it all seemed fine. He would show the results to my consultant but there did not seem anything to worry about. As the original mammogram was done by my local hospital, they did not have those original mammogram results to compare these with. I was allowed to dress and left the hospital. I burst into tears when I was alone with Roger, the relief was enormous. And how different it could have been if the results had been bad. I suppose I am going to feel this anxious every time I go for a check-up, and I am sure every woman who has had breast cancer feels the same.

I celebrated a year to the day since that dreadful news no woman should ever have to hear, with my family and pink champagne. Pink is the colour being used to promote cancer research into breast cancer, and charity support work by Marks & Spencer, and various other fund raising activities, including the 'Run For Life' organised sponsored runs all over the country. I am amazed by the support given to this type of fundraising ranging from young to old, women who have had breast cancer to children of those affected. It gives us all hope that one day this dreadful disease will be eradicated from our lives.

The final chapter for me was the nipple tattoo. This was the last bit of cosmetic treatment to make me able to face myself in the mirror and see a normal reflection. It had been four months since the nipple reconstruction and everything had settled down. I was looking forward to having the tattoo done before Christmas, so that I could start the New Year afresh. I had to go to a different hospital for this, an old military hospital further away. I was reassured to see the now familiar face of my consultant, who prepared me for the tattoo with local injections. He then used a colour chart to match up the flesh tones of my other nipple. A thought did flash through my mind to ask for a purple nipple as this is my favourite colour, but sobriety got the better of me and I kept quiet. He used a steam based gun and it took about half an hour. Waterproof plaster in place I left that hospital with a light heart. It was all done. A few days later I took the plaster off and was rather revolted by the sight of it! I was told it would all settle down in a couple of weeks which it did, in fact, although the nurse did say it would be darker at first, but it would go lighter in time. Good job I thought!

So that's that. It's done, it's over, the nightmare has ended. Fifteen months of my life has been blighted by this experience. I hope and pray it never returns. For the most part I am very positive. I still have times when I am convinced the cancer is back, in a different guise. My heart goes out to all of the women I hear about who have contracted breast cancer, and are about to go through, or are actually going through the ordeal of surgery and the various treatments. When I last saw my consultant he asked me if I would be prepared to speak to a patient of his who was about to embark on her surgery and needed someone to talk to, who had had the same surgery and treatment. He said I had a positive attitude and he was pleased with the reconstruction. I would be a good recommendation for the form of surgery and treatment we had chosen which was most appropriate for me. Speaking from personal experience, I would whole heartedly recommend reconstruction for women who have had to lose a breast. I can honestly say I do not look any different to you now. The scars have faded and the shape is good. I can wear whatever I choose and do whatever I like. I have been given my life back. How can you thank someone enough for that? To my oncologist, I owe you my life

It was time to get my personal life back on track. Looking at myself was difficult enough to accept. How would Roger feel when he saw me? When we first met it was all about my good body and he was a breast man so how would he feel now I had changed physically so much. I felt he would put on a brave face, but inwardly be shocked and reject me. He hadn't signed up for this!

I knew the time was coming when we would make love again. There was no going back to how it used to be. We were where we were. He told me afterwards, that the pressure on him had been building too, and he was very apprehensive, knowing his performance would be watched by me, for any repulsions or rejection, and he didn't want

any misinterpretation of lack of performance misconstrued by me as a rejection of his love for me.

One evening the opportunity arose for us to break down the barrier and see how things went. I needn't have worried. Roger was as loving and caring as always, if not more so. I felt every bit a woman and wasn't inhibited at all. Roger said he felt awful for all the time he used to say "I just love your breasts" now knowing half of me was reconstruction and senseless. Well that was then and now was now. I hadn't changed as a person. My consultant had done a brilliant job, even realigning my normal breast to match! This was as perfect as it could be. The only thing that had changed was any sensitivity, which was my problem to deal with, and I still had one normal breast. I was lucky. Women who had double mastectomies must have had so much more to deal with.

I would recommend reconstruction immediately after mastectomy. I knew if I could get back most of what I'd lost, my self-esteem and confidence would come back. I would be able to wear anything with confidence. It was important to me to still feel attractive, and I did. Soon this became a natural part of me. I was so grateful that the reconstruction was as good as it was. It gave me back my life.

A New Career

Almost at the same time while all this was happening we moved house. To understand why on earth we did that while all this was going on, I need to explain what had been happening in our lives in the meantime. When I got breast cancer, we were living in a beautiful dwelling with my girls and two dogs. We were so happy; a dream home with wooden floors and huge exposed beams, with an open fireplace and a swimming pool leading off of the master bedroom. Times were good, and life was a breeze; Roger's daughter wanted to live with us and it didn't seem to be a financial problem to have a large extension built into the house to accommodate her. Well as is often the case, the building works were seriously hampered by builders, bad weather, and a multitude of other problems which delayed the completion of the works by about eighteen months! Roger's daughter did come to live with us, but for such a short while, it made a mockery of the expense of it all. It was during this interim period that I contracted cancer. Our world was shot to pieces. At the same time Roger's business had taken a huge blow. The company he was working for went under, and we were left with a huge mortgage and mounting debts. It was six months after I had been given the all clear, that we realised we were not coping financially. Time to move to a place where we could gather ourselves and deal with our financial problems. We moved to a perfectly adequate town house and started anew.

It was October 2008 and I was working nearly full time as a PA and office manager at a fine dining restaurant. I have never known such a transient business as the restaurant business. Staff starting their job and then leaving on a whim, with absolutely no regard whatsoever for loyalty and dedication to the job! It became increasingly obvious that the restaurant was beginning to suffer too. Bad management, poor organisation, ever increasing costs, horrendous overheads and a restaurateur who spent more time distracted by his own private life than running a business, meant the staff did what they liked, and gradually there was a slow decline into eventual closure.

During the four years I had worked at the restaurant, I had come to realise that if I was ever going to make something of my life, I had to find something to do for myself. I began contemplating becoming a hypnotherapist and counsellor. I had always been interested in psychology and intrigued at how our minds work, and of course my own experiences with hypnotherapy. Yes it would mean studying again, and it was a long time since I had done any of that! But the prospect of doing something really meaningful that would also change other people's lives for the better would give me a sense of purpose, and reward. I was into college for three years, part time, so I could keep my job at the restaurant too which was vital for our income. For most of the students who decide to take up hypnotherapy and counselling, they themselves have had one or both therapies in their life, and have benefitted from it; and I of course was no exception.

The information I am about to impart I have only ever told four people about until now . . . The first was my first husband John, who had no idea of the severity of my condition; the second was my second husband Richard, who supported me and allowed me to find my way back to normality with a hypnotherapist's help . . . and the third Roger, who has been the constant source of support and understanding throughout the whole journey.

At the age of 17 years old, I developed Agoraphobia. It took over my life.

My Introduction To Hypnotherapy

When I was eighteen years old, I had my first panic attack. This was a very scary event. I began having panic attacks with alarming regularity. Over a period of eight years, my world got smaller and smaller. I stopped going to places where I had attacks; stopped going out of my comfort zone. I was a classic agoraphobic. I told no one except my boyfriend, who couldn't understand it at all. It felt like I was a weak person having this phobia, but for those who have ever suffered from panic attacks, facing the fear every day of your life, still doing what you had to do, that is not being weak. My anxiety levels got worse and worse and I was in a constant state of fear.

I was in a steady relationship and for want of a better expression, I was bored. We had been together several years, and I believed the next natural step was to get married. Well that would give me something to preoccupy myself with, planning and arranging a wedding! Having said that, it was one of the hardest things I faced, standing at the altar of a big church, knowing all of those people were watching me, just wishing I could run home and hide in the safety of my bedroom. The honeymoon was equally as terrorising, on a motorbike, on a long ferry crossing which was delayed at sea during a storm, to an island where the only way back was to retrace our steps.

After six months of marriage . . . I was still quite young, only 20 years old . . . the dim prospect of spending all my life with this man was beginning to depress me. I wasn't ready to settle down but was too damn frightened to do anything about it. But something inside me began to rebel. I was being stifled by a possessive jealous husband. So it came to the point when it took a lot of engineering just to organise a night out with a girlfriend. He interrogated me before we went out, where we were going, what we would be doing, it was making me more determined to have a good time and forget I was married.

So I decided to change the course of my future one evening. My girlfriend and I hit the local nightclub and I was in party mode. I knew an old flame was a bouncer there, although he wasn't working that evening, and I asked one of his friends to be sure to tell him I was asking after him and would like to see him. At the time it was a bit of drunken devilment, but a part of me did want to meet. It wasn't long before he made contact with me at work. We met up, and I knew I could still have him if I wanted. We began meeting whenever we could and I soon knew I had to end what was a very short marriage, and be free again. With the courage and strength it took to dissolve that marriage, my agoraphobia began to recede. And it did take some courage. My husband wasn't going without a fight. In his imagination, he had already concluded I was sleeping with my old flame and I had been having an affair for a while, and he worked himself up to such a frenzy, he came at me with a knife and I was cornered in the bathroom, terrified. All his rationality gone, he broke down. I don't know where the inner strength came from for me, but a determined coldness had taken over me, and I began to face life without him as my security blanket.

Well at the risk of repeating myself . . . and history repeating itself . . . I got settled into another steady relationship, and within two years I was ready to marry again. Spurred on by being back living with my parents, who's own relationship was volatile to say the least, and still that agoraphobia lurking in the background, I wanted security and adoration, and I was getting it in spades. My second husband was a good, loyal, kind man. And he loved me. We set up home in a small two up two down terraced house, and were very happy, apart from the agoraphobia which wasn't going away. It began to dawn on me that I needed some help.

I looked in the local paper and found a hypnotherapist called Kathleen Ayres in the Personal Ads. I plucked up the courage to ring her and arranged to go to her house for a session. Even getting to her house a few miles away was an ordeal for me. I arrived with palms sweating, heart racing, knees shaking; it was ridiculous but I couldn't stop it. She was a softly spoken woman and I relaxed a little. We began what transpired to be two years of sessions before I was able to see my way forward on my own, and years of self-doubt after that. I had had this phobia for 12 years and it took a long time to unravel the deep-seated fear. At the time I didn't know if this person was authentic, and even to this day there is not enough protection in place for the patients.

Hypnotherapists still battle against the old beliefs that they are weird, spooky, controlling and frightening, manipulating people into doing dark deeds. There is however much more credence given to hypnotherapy as a valuable alternative therapy to pills from the doctor. Nevertheless we still have a long way to go in convincing GPs that it IS an alternative to antidepressants which they are so keen to dish out to alleviate symptoms, even if they don't cure the problem.

What can I say? It took two years of hypnotherapy, and she discovered I had a balance problem (even then), which could be rectified with exercises, and I should see a consultant she knew in London. The thought of travelling to London filled me with dread even with Richard driving the car, but we went . . . I was tested thoroughly and sent away to do the exercises and correct my posture. When I was small I walked with one instep turned down although I can't remember which foot and no parent here to ask, and I remember going to the local War Memorial Hospital regularly to correct it; I was taught to write with my feet, pick things up and had one shoe built up to get my posture right. This may have had a bearing on this latest diagnosis.

Where Did It All Come From?

I wondered how much of my past had affected me, as a child growing up in an environment where I was the go-between for my parents when they were living apart, and I was part private detective, creeping around alleyways, to see if my dad's car was parked outside one of his mistresses houses. There were many tears and shouting, breaking up and making up, then another affair would start . . . and so it began again.

My Dad went to his grave in shame, and enormous debt. My Mum had to sell the family house and lived alone for the remainder of her life. She had truly loved that man. She was buried in the same grave. She won him for ever in death. I hated him for what he had done to our family, and I hated him for dying and leaving my mum in such a mess. His latest squeeze even turned up at the funeral. Little did I know I would be breaking hearts, and splitting families up when it came to my turn. It's easy in hindsight and after life experience to feel differently about it all, but at the time I was naïve and protective of my mother. I will never know why he did what he did, and there's always two sides to every story isn't there? He died at the steering wheel of his van. He'd had a heart attack. He was 57 years old. He smoked 40 non tipped Senior Service cigarettes a day and coughed for England. The stress of his lifestyle alone was enough to kill him. If I could see him again, I might understand the man better and I regret not having the chance to have that conversation with him. An older work colleague said to me once, "your dad is a good looking man!" Funny I had never seen it. He was just my Dad.

I remember one time when my mum had just discovered another affair and my parents were arguing, going at it hammer and tongs, in what we used to call the breakfast room. It was a room off a very small kitchen where the seven of us ate our meals. My mum, bless her, was not a great cook; not even a good one. It was something she had to do and a lot of it she did. My mum's generation more often than not massacred vegetables, used cheap cuts of meat and everything tasted bland. She was in fact at the time preparing one of her culinary delights and about to lay the table with seven plates. She was a soft, kind, loving woman, but she lost her temper with my dad that day, and in a fit of rage threw all the dinner plates at him in one go! I don't know where she found the strength to lift them above her head first, let alone throw them. He ducked, and they smashed to pieces against the wall. Dinner was on "afters" plates that night.

Sometimes Mum would confide in me about him, during the times when she was angry, lonely, overworked and trying to keep a house going on her own. She recalled to me once she was doing the housework and the doorbell rang. When she answered it a brazen woman was standing on the steps and looking puzzled at my mother, asked, "Who are you?" to which my mother replied, "Mrs Rawson, who are you?" She replied, "I am Vince's fiancée." I wasn't there to witness that event, I only know that not long after, I saw my mother standing with her hat and coat on, the front door open, suitcases in hand, debating should she go or should she stay. My brother and sisters were all crying, begging her to stay. And she did, and we never knew what an unhappy life she was living.

My dad was a character. He was from Dukinfield in Lancashire, and was brought up by his grandmother. His mother died when he was still young. She had suffered from severe chest problems, brought about from working in the cotton mills. He was taught the piano and loved it. He played to a very high standard, and my brother and sisters learned our love of classical music from him. But as he grew up, he realised his natural skill for finding a tune on the piano was to stand him in good stead, playing at night in the local pubs. He wasn't a drinker and a half of beer would see him right all night. But he did have an eye for the ladies, and partly this is where he would have his fun. Don't get me wrong. He worked all day in a local factory. He wasn't a shirker. And he did have to make ends meet, by working in the pubs too, because my mum wanted the best start in life for us kids, and she insisted we all went to private school to get a good education; and that cost money! And anything we really wanted to do or learn, they found the money for us to do it. On reflection, it was no wonder he struggled to keep their heads above water. Because of his piano skills, he would teach the piano too . . . another temptation for him when the mother of the pupil was attractive, one in particular as I recall, who lived in a road parallel to ours, joined by a footpath. When my mother suspected him of having an affair with her, she took me down the footpath and sent me round the corner to see if his car was parked down her road . . . and it was. Hardly hiding the fact! It would be interesting to hear his mistress's account of him. Another use of his piano skills was playing the organ at our local church. He was brought up a strict Catholic, and so it followed we all went to a Catholic school. Whilst we all had to toe the line as far as the nuns were concerned, and go to church every Sunday, high day and holiday, and say our prayers, we didn't consider ourselves a religious family. And my dad was by no means a religious man. He played the organ at the church because he got paid. It gave him recognition too, which meant he played at all the weddings which were held there, and—again—got paid. But what confirmed for me that he was not a respectful catholic, was once when I went up the winding creaky wooden stairs to where the organ was at the back of the church, to find him smoking, and reading the paper, with the choir taking no notice of him whatsoever. Obviously a regular occurrence! At that moment the church bell rang to say the priest was coming out, and he hurriedly stamped out his cigarette, threw the paper to the floor and starting playing the organ! Not acceptable these days.

He was a smooth talker. I remember once, in his painting and decorating days, when he tendered for a refurbishment job at the largest hotel in our home town and somehow got the job. What they didn't know: he was a one man band! It was a huge undertaking. He roped us all in to help and we didn't know the first thing about redecoration, let alone plastering. It was a nightmare! He must have had sleepless nights over it. But in hindsight he was doing his best to earn enough to keep his large family going, the only way he knew how.

My family were so important to me, my three sisters and brother, and their respective halfs. We all got on so well, Even more so since my parents have died years ago now. We would all get together and have fun. My mother outlived my dad for twenty years, but unfortunately she developed Alzheimer's and was constantly accusing us of all sorts of things. We ignored it all of course, and looked after her as best we could, with our own families to look after too. My Mum died in 2002. I was 46 years old. She had oesophageal cancer which was inoperable. She had Alzheimer's disease to an extent, so mercifully was not fully aware of what was happening to her. She could still manage to live on her own, but her kitchen was wall to wall post-its and notes on scraps of paper and old envelopes reminding her of every-day tasks. She would misplace things and then accuse us all of stealing them. My youngest sister Christina and my sister Debra's partner Phil were usually the "culprits". We all took it in good heart because of her condition, however there was one occasion when Phil decided to play a practical joke on Christina, and in no way reflected on our mum. The latest obsession my mum had at the time, was to accuse Christina of stealing her nighties. It became a standing joke with the rest of us. There was no way she would have stolen mum's old winceyette nighties! Phil worked in a garage at the time, and they were often given old rags to wipe their hands on etc. In one bag he received there were a lot of old nighties. To keep our mums life simple, Christina, Debra and I would have her over on certain days of the week. Phil knew what day she visited Christina, so he surreptitiously went over to Christina's house, and while my sister was out collecting mum, he pegged all the old nighties on her washing line. When she arrived at home with mum, and mum saw them all on the line, she firmly believed they were hers and here was the proof! Christina was horrified, and had to placate mum with tea and cake, when she instantly forgot about it all, but it took Christina a while to find out what had happened. She was not amused! We all laughed, which was sometimes the only way of dealing with the worry and sadness we all felt for her.

The Schaefers

*I*n 2009 we met the Schaefers who became our very good friends. One day Roger was walking our dogs Gin and Saffi down at Pagham Nature Reserve as he did every morning, when his path crossed with a lady and her dogs. He got talking to her, and asked why she had her dogs on a lead. She said because we had to according to the warden. Roger scoffed and said if the dogs were ok with other animals they should be having a run. This was to be the start of an amazing friendship. They walked and talked. Jeannette had come over from Germany a few years ago to live permanently in the UK. She spent her time, mostly on her own with her Golden Retriever Sam and her rescue crossbreed Jill. Her husband Ruediger works in Germany and only comes home at the weekends and for holidays.

One day Roger and Jeannette bumped into each other again dog walking, and he asked her if she worked. She said she was doing a Hypnotherapy Course in Chichester. "How bizarre" he said, "Vivienne has just completed a Hypnotherapy Course in Worthing," and it turned out we had done the same course at different venues with the same company! When he told me about Jeannette, I said maybe we will get together and chat about it sometime.

It wasn't until Boxing Day 2009, at the traditional local Pram Race in Pagham, that I met Jeannette and we briefly talked about the hypnotherapy course. I said if she wanted any help, or to do some practice to get in touch, especially as she hardly knew anyone around here, having recently moved from Germany to the UK.

Well she did get in touch, and we began to formulate what has turned out to be the strongest female relationship I have ever had. We found we had so much in common, especially party time!! In due course we met Jeannette's husband Ruediger (English translation is Roger!). We began socialising with them, and found them to be great company. Ruediger works for an international insurance company, despite qualifying as a Doctor of Law. He was a prosecuting lawyer, but couldn't stand the details of the crimes he was prosecuting against, and decided to go for a complete change of career. He is extremely successful in his field of work, and such a gentleman.

We had some great times with them, including a birthday bash we held at home for Roger, when we asked our 10 dinner guests to come dressed up, using a theme of Music Genres. Ruediger came as Elvis, and Jeannette as Amy Winehouse, complete with tattoos, cigarette hanging from her mouth, and a wig to die for! We had a hysterical evening, and it sealed the fate of a great friendship. Roger and Ruediger got on famously too, a rare thing for all four in two couples to get on so well

Jeannette and I were beginning to gel so well together as friends, and also with our huge interest in hypnotherapy. I was getting to the point where treating at home was not enough for me, and she became very interested in the idea of joining forces and setting up a therapy centre for hypnotherapy and counselling. We began to hatch a plan and start looking for premises. We very soon were lucky enough to find the perfect place, near where we both lived. It would take some doing up and quite a large amount of capital, but Jeannette formulated a sound business plan and we were very confident of the huge success this was going to be. We set about the new business in October 2010 and we were just about ready to start the new business in the new year. We had a great welcoming party with friends and family to show off the bespoke premises, all done tastefully and professionally. We designed packages for group programmes for weight loss, business programmes, and other incentives to encourage people to address their issues, and set to work practising on willing family and friends in readiness.

How Life Changes

*J*anuary 4th 2011. The first day of practice at our new Therapy Centre! We marched in with huge pride and enthusiasm. Day one of what we hoped would be a glowing success. As I unlocked the door I felt a bit off balance which seemed strange. I guessed it was probably the excitement of our new venture.

Gin, our massive, passive, adorable German Shepherd was behaving oddly. The vet said he would run some tests and ring us later. I had left him going off for a walk, and on his return Roger said he kept sitting down on the walk. Unheard of. When Roger took him to the vet I said flippantly, "Mind you bring him back now" . . . I didn't know I was never going to see Gin again. They performed surgery on him for a Splenic tumour and found he was riddled with cancer. I knew that teatime, we had the final call, but that was one of the hardest days of my life. Later that day my beautiful dog Gin died. He had cancer . . . He had been so special to me. It was such a shock. I felt so sad . . .

I continued to work and become proactive about the business marketing. Saffi (short for Sapphire as in Bombay Sapphire Gin) our ugly Staffi missed Gin terribly. She would just sit on her bed with the blanket resting on her nose, miserable, without her playmate. They say you should show the remaining pet the dead animal for acceptance, but as that wasn't possible, she was pining, confused and lonely.

Late January saw the adoption of a new friend for Saffi; a young male GSD called Max . . . Well we had to keep the gin theme up so we changed that to Miller . . . a very reputable gin . . . He liked his new name and his new home. Saffi's loneliness was over . . . if only all of life was that easy. If it's broken get a new one! It didn't repair my heart but Miller has filled a gap in our lives. We got him through The Kennel Club GSD Rescue Centre. There were 32 dogs waiting to be rehomed. How sad. Actually there were only four which fitted the bill as far as we were concerned. We had to take Saffi for her approval of course . . . and then there was one she met which seemed to fit the bill! She 'chose' Miller, I say that guardedly, and at times in the first few weeks I am sure she questioned her judgement, as did we!

I developed a cough and a bit of a headache, but with so many viruses around, coupled with feelings of loss, pressure to make the new business work, and growing financial pressures at home, it was no wonder I was feeling stressed.

As January wore on I noticed I was finding it more and more difficult to keep my balance. I noticed too that the shooting headache at the back of my head was increasingly worse. By Sunday 30th January I felt dreadful. The pain in my head made me vomit, and I keeled over on the bathroom floor.

The paramedics made me walk to the ambulance in my dressing gown for all to see! And so I began the process of being in A & E, slowly followed by an Assessment Medical Ward, with nurses and doctors all taking notes, doing the same tests, and every single time the same questions, can you tell me your name and date of birth. I know they have a job to do but really . . . I hadn't moved, I was still in the same space . . . why would I be a different person? I was put into a general ward next and offered some painkillers . . . the poor nurses were so over-worked; the pills arrived an hour and a half later. Roger persevered with getting me moved to the Private Suite as we were on BUPA, and at 9pm I arrived to my room and promptly vomited everywhere. A kind but abrupt tall doctor did his rounds at 12.10am, woke me and asked lots of questions . . . He said "you seem confused" . . . So would he if he had just been woken up to answer staccato questions as to times, dates, events etc!

Monday was my introduction to Mr Holman, my on-hand consultant, although a Colon cancer specialist. He arrived with an entourage of students all eagerly asking questions. I was surprised he hadn't asked my permission but I didn't mind . . . He said I needed a CAT scan. He asked me what I did, and I told him briefly . . . He patted his stomach after I told him about my hypnotic gastric band programme. I merely said "We'll talk later". The day passed, Roger persuaded the nurse to let an auxiliary nurse wheel me down to the outside for a cigarette. They were brilliant! Monday evening Mr Holman was back in my room, the news was not what I was expecting. He said there was something in my Cerebellum—a 4cm tumour. Shock . . . that cold tingly feeling you get creeping round your body when shock takes over. More scans to give a clearer picture were needed, namely an MRI brain scan. I used to be very claustrophobic, and having not really tested myself out in a very stressful situation, he said I could have a sedative before it. Relief!

Tuesday I was scheduled for another CAT scan from my neck down, followed by an MRI head scan, the dreaded tube, later in the day. I duly arrived at the scanning unit to be told that while I was there they may as well do the MRI straight after the CAT scan. My eyes opened widely and I asked about the sedative. Half hour later they said they couldn't do the scan till later that day or even Wednesday as there was no doctor available to do the sedation. I said' let's get on with it then' . . . and so it was done . . . and I coped far better than I ever would have before I learned about hypnotherapy. I coped fine.

Back on the ward, saw Mr Holman again and he said I could go home. He did a test on me, making me march on the spot with my arms outstretched and eyes shut. You would ordinarily stay on the spot but I turned 180 degrees! This was quite a shock to me. I was glad to go home. We had missed out on the Sunday I was admitted to hospital on a fabulous Sunday Club luncheon. Eight of us get together every three months or so and have an amazing lunch, copious amounts of wine and much laughter. It was our friends Kathy and Brian's turn. They used to run a pub, and she makes the most amazing Steak and Ale pie. Roger was very upset not to tuck lots of that away. Ah well . . . we were to miss even greater times. The weekend following my return home we should have been in Stuttgart in Southern Germany! It was Ruediger's 50th birthday event, and they were treating us to a long weekend of celebrations. What a shame to miss that! I had bought a new dress too.

Home to tell my girls what was next for me. They were so good, so positive . . . such lovely girls!

In the next few days, I began to work out what I could be doing for myself, now I knew the diagnosis. Funny enough Jeannette was doing the same. Having learned this amazing mental tool of hypnotherapy, and the power of the subconscious mind, I knew there were ways of creating a healing process for myself, using the power of my mind and kick-starting my immune system into destroying the cancerous cells. Jeannette appeared on the doorstep with some books. She had been rummaging around our books at the Therapy Centre and came across a book we had both read when we were doing our course in Hypnotherapy, called "The Power of Your Subconscious Mind" by Dr Joseph Murphy. Reading it again, I was inspired, incredulous, totally overwhelmed by the accuracy of his book, and how it would help me change my life. I set to work immediately writing myself scripts and recording them onto my Blackberry to listen to before I went to sleep, and again on waking up. Throughout the day I repeated positive affirmations to myself. 'I am in perfect health . . . I am successful . . . I am wealthy . . . my infinitely powerful subconscious mind knows how to heal me . . . I am recreating the blueprint of a perfect body . . .' Did you know our body is totally renewed over 11 months? I didn't. So within 11 months almost every cell in our bodies has been renewed.

It was phenomenal the difference self-hypnosis made to my attitude, my way of being, and how I dealt with everything. No one could believe how positive I was being, taking it all in my stride, not worrying at all. I felt like I was having the best time, that holiday feeling, so happy and relaxed;

family and friends could not get over how I was being. What a profound effect this book had had on me. My personal journey with hypnosis changed my life. I read probably the first 80 pages . . . all the information I needed was here in this book. It was so significant for me. And vital changes took place within me on phenomenal level.

There were other major changes happening in my life . . . and all at the same time!

The debts kept mounting. Roger is a tool designer and finding new work was a struggle. Our country was feeling the pinch, as it went into a recession. It was another blow for us to cope with. We had barely managed for 5 years, until the debts overtook us in the end and Roger was made bankrupt. Our house was going to be repossessed and we had to find somewhere to rent.

Roger and I had a conversation with my girls about moving house. They were going to have to go back to their Dad's to live, and Roger and I plus dogs were going to rent a property for the time being. Our great friends the Schaefer's came to our rescue. They decided to buy a property and let it to us. Their generosity was overwhelming. We were involved right from the start, making sure we would be happy, and they would have a sound investment. Well it was all happening at once. I was in and out of hospital for various scans, xrays, appointments, and in the meantime we were viewing houses with our friends We viewed 21 houses and bungalows. The ball was rolling on the first property we found we liked, but due to structural problems we pulled out. The second one we chose became complicated with the amount of work it would need to make it habitable, but the third one seem to suit us all. It would mean some "minor" doing up but it was doable. Well what began as a small project developed into a much larger one of course. The bathroom was ripped out, likewise the kitchen, and eventually the whole place was gutted and we started again. Roger did a lot of the work himself to keep costs down, but it was a gruelling three months before it was ready enough to move into. We moved on the 23rd of July 2011—a date in between my chemotherapy appointments when I felt energetic enough to cope. It seemed very strange at first, especially as I was in and out of hospital, and only there for a few nights at a time. It didn't feel like home for some while. I still remember when it was my youngest daughter's 21st birthday, and we celebrated the following day with cake and champagne at our new abode, but part of me was so sad that they wouldn't be living with us anymore. Usually it's the children that flee the nest, but in this instance it was us! They would be okay. My eldest set up in a flat with her boyfriend, and the younger two moved in with their dad.

Back to February 2011 It was Valentine's Day. And how romantic . . . an appointment with my oncologist in the evening. I didn't feel the least bit romantic. He informed me I will have an operation in Southampton General Hospital in about two weeks' time. Sure enough two weeks later I am scheduled for the operation. I duly go there for my pre-operation assessment and another MRI scan . . . only 8 minutes this time . . . but how my self-hypnosis helped!!!! It was amazing how good I felt. And while we were waiting to see various staff in various departments we looked around and people-watched in this very busy hospital . . . We were horrified at the amount of people, patients AND staff who are morbidly obese. It was quite remarkable that there were far more fat people than people of normal build. Everywhere we looked there were very fat people. There is something going really wrong with our diet these days. It was SO noticeable. It was actually awful to see so many fat people labouring as they walked, puffing and panting . . . and that was just the staff! I could see the potential for my hypnotic gastric band programme everywhere!

However I am told the operation will not be the following week Monday 21 Feb as the neurosurgeon is so busy and needs a break, having done numerous operations and been on call, he would not be safe wielding a scalpel at 7.30am on a Monday morning! I agree he would have to be accurate, so the operation is rearranged for the Friday 25th February. And I wait.

Meanwhile, I continued to treat clients and did not let on what was happening to me. The steroids I had to take to keep the tumour under control until the surgery, were keeping me very busy! A drug called Dexamethasone, they kept me hyperactive for up to 21 hours a day! I filled my time on my laptop, and baking cakes then eating them! My appetite was huge. I was gaining weight every day.

In that interim period I received many cards. It was interesting to see the cards which plopped through my letterbox that week from extended family and friends. The lack of knowledge about these things half scares people to death. It's strange how people perceive things so differently, and of course that depends on their state of mind. Some cards were in the category of 'Thinking of you at this time . . .' like someone had died! I threw those away. One card which gave me hope was a hand delivered good luck card containing kind words from my ex-husband; a break-through on the contact front, but why it should have come to this before he put pen to paper is all too sad to contemplate. He was still so angry and it had been 12 years since we had split up.

It was Friday 25th February 2011. Operation day dawns . . . no food or drink for me. We have to be at Southampton at 7.30am. I am stripped of day clothes, and lay on a bed, and am immediately institutionalised.

Various blood tests and examinations later I finally get to meet my neurosurgeon . . . Mr Paul Grundy. He approached Roger and me, and we thought he was the Anaesthetist. He looked about 25 but was probably nearer 30 years old. Good God, did he know enough to be rooting around in my brain? Well he was treated like a God at the hospital so I knew he was the main man for the job.

He said the neurosurgery unit was so busy with emergencies, he really wasn't sure I would get my operation that day either, but it could be rescheduled to the following Wednesday at the private hospital over the road. Whilst the private bit tempted me, I really wanted to get this over with now I had come this far. He said he would make some phone calls, and at 1.20pm, came flying in and said, "We're on!" He then had to make us aware by law, of the possible complications I may have, and also the percentage chances of negative effects of the surgery! Well I had convinced myself I was almost going in for an ingrowing toe nail type of small operation but that information scared me. He said there was a 10 to 15% chance I could have facial paralysis, I immediately thought no I'm not having that . . . And on and on he went . . . and at everything he said I told myself . . . 'No I'm not having that either . . .' He did say it wasn't going to be straightforward and the operation may take up to six hours. Six hours? What on earth was he doing in there for six hours? Well the seriousness of it all suddenly hit home but I had no time to think about it. They came to get me.

And off I went. Roger left after a brief goodbye and good luck. We could barely look at each other. This was it . . . and I was whisked away to theatre. No pre-med . . . it makes recovery quicker. I was busy giving the anaesthetist information about hypnotherapy when within seconds I was out cold. I woke up in recovery and was told it was very successful and only took 3.5 hours. The neurosurgeon rang Roger to say the tumour came away surprisingly easily. I wonder why? The hypnotherapy was working! Undoubtedly you can make material changes to your physical life, and save yourself. I'd had since Wednesday 2nd February to work on my self-hypnosis—I recorded a session onto my ipod and played it every night and every morning. I kept improving the session to give it more depth. I used my positive affirmations many times a day, reconditioning my subconscious mind to believe I was going to be well again. I was able to get myself into such a good place mentally, I had even forgotten I was about to have major life-saving surgery. I was so positive everyone remarked on it. I expect they felt I had lost the plot, but I was more focused than ever before that I was going to be fine.

My recovery from the brain tumour was swift and brilliant. I was in the top neurological unit in the South of England, with the top neurosurgeon. It was a general hospital and extremely busy! I was on the ITU ward and it was frantic . . . like you see on TV . . . organised chaos . . . no peace . . . . My inmates had various traumas while I was there, one patient dislodged her canula from her foot and blood was spurting everywhere at 1.30am; not much sleep for anyone that night! As is always the case with hospital food, it was vile. Just thinking about it makes me want to vomit even now. Curry and rice . . . I was so sick . . . . The staff were so overstretched, it was Roger who held the bowl for me, held my head and cleaned me up. What a job . . . not what he signed up for all those years ago when we started our passionate affair. Day 4 was the bedbath. What fun that was. I just wanted to be left in dirt and squalor but no, hygiene comes first. And the days began to pass quicker; the spinal drain was removed and I was instructed by the physiotherapist that I had to demonstrate sitting, walking, doing stairs etc before I could be discharged. That gave me the determination to perform! Sleep deprivation was the worst, and my neighbour June, kept setting off her drip alarm which I could have happily stabbed her for!

I was finally allowed to leave the hospital, having had 22 metal clips removed from my head, which were keeping my brain inside! Lots of R & R at home, I tried to do my self-hypnosis but the steroids were inhibiting it and I couldn't relax. Roger managed to organise for me to be transferred by private ambulance to our local hospital to the private suite as an interim measure. I was so grateful to be out of the general hospital.

I spent the next two weeks recovering at home, but all too soon I faced the next phase of my treatment, radiology. This was an experience I was glad to get past, although I wonder how I would have got through it so well without the self-hypnosis. I hated the idea of the MRI scan, in a tunnel. Claustrophobia was one of my biggest fears. I trained my mind, in those two weeks to detach myself from my situation and take myself to a wonderful place of escapism, while I had the vital treatment. Sometimes it's better not to know what is coming. I was totally unprepared for the mask. I was taken into a room to have a mask made of my head and face, which is then used to keep my head completely still while the 5 minute radio waves were sent into my head. It was like something out of a horror movie. I was laid down and the mask was fixed to the treatment bed, locking my head in position. If you have ever suffered from claustrophobia, the thought of this will petrify you. I have suffered from claustrophobia, and was amazed at my control and calm when I was led through this process . . . 5 days in a row.

It was quite strange. I continued to treat clients, one of which that particular week, informed me she had just been diagnosed with breast cancer and was afraid of what she was about to face. I detached myself from my own circumstances, and was able to fully support her, and treat her with all the knowledge I had to make her journey the smoothest possible. She and her husband were totally amazed at her new behaviour after a few sessions of hypnotherapy.

The radiotherapy was successful. I used all the powers within myself to talk myself into the healing white light that was penetrating my head, and how good it felt to wear the mask, because it was helping me. I was healing rapidly. I would never have cancer again. This self-hypnosis would help so many people. It was my defining role to teach this to as many people who would learn it, to help themselves.

I had to try and get myself better quickly and continue my work. I was advised to reconnect the neurons of my brain, by working on my balance. I tried riding my daughter's bike in trepidation. I was nervous in case I lost my balance and my confidence would go. What would life be like if I couldn't stay balanced? The first few circuits of the pedals were slow and shaky but gradually I got faster and was so happy to be cycling, free and independent. This was particularly important as, due to an unwavering law of the DVLA, if you have had a brain tumour, you are automatically banned from driving a car for at least a year, just in case you suffer from an epileptic fit. My surgeon said that this sort of brain tumour would not cause epilepsy, however his neck was on the line if something had happened in that first year. So my licence was removed and I was without a car. I couldn't help but feel resentful that not only my life was being changed as a result of poor health, but all the things I took for granted were being taken away from me too. I resolved not to wallow in self-pity, and went straight out and bought myself a new bike. Well if this was going to be my main form of independent transport, I might as well enjoy it!

A Question Of Balance

4th April 2011, and no more pills to take. The steroids had done their job. Unfortunately so had the radiotherapy in that, as the hospital explained, I would lose my hair as a result. And despite a delay in that happening, it did happen. Well I have lost all my hair before, and it all came back perfectly okay. I still had the wig in the loft. Now a part of me wonders if when I put that wig in the loft 4.5 years ago, was I expecting to have to wear it again at some point in the future. Had I been preparing myself to have cancer again without consciously knowing it? Had I talked myself into it? It was an eerie feeling to think I may have in some way been responsible for my ill health, simply by not contemplating it, it may not have happened. Do we really have the power to control that? And if we do why didn't someone tell me about it! Shouldn't the NHS and all the powers be promoting the use of hypnosis for everyone to empower themselves, to help heal themselves, to control their fears. Shouldn't there be available, all the help we can get regarding coping with the problems we are faced with. What about promoting the use of hypnosis to help patients with treatments they have to face, for example MRI scans. We should be in awe of our mind. It is infinitely powerful. We only touch the surface of its power. If we can unlock its power, there are no limits to what we can achieve.

Scarily, a regular CT scan some weeks later showed lung and liver tumours! I was again shocked and bewildered how this could be happening. More chemotherapy followed; it was becoming acceptable to me, or rather I was getting used to the regime of it. I continued avidly with my self hypnosis.

It was when I had the results of the next CT scan, that I began to realise my internal power was far more than I knew. The oncologist said the 2 lung tumours had stabilised; the liver tumour had shrunk. Could this be because of my self-hypnosis? I had been working on controlling and shrinking the tumours in my affirmations. Well something was working, and I hadn't been given any pills for it. The oncologist was surprised and mystified by the turn around in the behaviour of the tumours. I was still in line for chemotherapy, and was prepared to allow that to take place, covering all angles.

It's 19th April 2011, and so it began again; a round of consultations, blood tests, xrays, followed by drip fed toxic liquid into my ever failing and collapsing veins. The list of side effects was long, and taking that into consideration, I didn't suffer too badly. But it's true that the brute strength of the chemicals used to kill the cancer, will inevitably have an effect on the healthy cells too. The usual chronic fatigue, aches and pains were there every time, as was the marked change in taste. Everything including water tasted vile for the first 10 days or so, then there was a gradual return to nearly normal, but then I was off again on the next round of chemo. I tried to use my self-hypnosis to correct the taste buds, but I did struggle to make a difference. I couldn't concentrate on the hypnosis anyway due to the steroids making my mind buzz all of the time. When I was able to get myself into a hypnotic state, I used suggestions to my subconscious mind to shrink the tumours in my lungs and liver, and bring myself back to perfect health.

Helping Myself

Mid-year 2011 was upon us already. I was facing two operations for micro-ablation surgery and two more sets of chemotherapy. We managed to take a short break away in our sweet little caravan to a quiet site near Salisbury. Believe me don't knock it till you've tried it. We had such fun on those holidays. When the weather was good we walked for miles, when the weather was bad we cosied up and read books. We barbequed a lot, coupled with much partaking of the wine, with our favourite music on the ipod. It was great escapism. What I would say though, is you should like the person you are sharing home with, because it is very cosy inside. And there is quite a lot of packing up, travelling and for us, with dogs, pee stops, and setting up takes two hours or so. But that first glass of wine tastes all the sweeter once the work is all done! We only had a few days for me between hospital visits, and I returned to face my next battle.

My dear friend Jeannette had come across a book called "Anti-Cancer—a new way of life" by Dr David Servan-Schreiber. She gave me a copy and said 'read it and do it'. It was quite a learning curve for me. I had no idea refined sugar is more dangerous to our bodies, more than nicotine or alcohol; white flour, white pasta, white rice and dairy products are bad for our bodies too. As I began to take this on board, and started to look at what I actually did consume, it was clear to me we had been eating a lot of 'bad' foods, and worse, I had ignorantly fed my children according to my Western diet too. It was only when diseases were brought to our attention on the TV or in the newspapers, that we learned for example that salt is very bad for high blood pressure, can trigger heart attacks and strokes. Sugar is one of the main contributors of diabetes, obesity, strokes etc. If we went back to how our ancestors ate, the Caveman diet of berries, fruit, vegetables and occasional meat or fish, there would be none of these modern diseases. Charged with all this new information, Roger went off to the supermarket to do the food shopping, only to realise that almost everything that is processed in any way has sugar in it. I was shocked. Even sauces, pastes, bread, meats, even accompaniments to meats have sugar in them. It makes a mockery of the Government, who are 'looking out for the nations' health, that there aren't tighter controls in what is made available in the shops for us to choose from in the first place. Surely that isn't rocket science! Your average person does not shop by looking at every label to see what the ingredients are. It took Roger and I four hours to do the shopping that week! And we didn't come away with anything much that went together because a lot of what we had picked up, we had put back on the shelf. We arrived home to find we had such a strange mix of foods, we didn't have the right ingredients to make one single dinner! We started trying to find healthful recipes incorporating our new found healthy purchases, and discovered it took a further few hours before anything respectable had made it's way onto our dinner plates. This suggests we had an awful diet before these revelations, but that simply wasn't true. We did eat reasonably healthily, and made a lot of our own dishes, but there is nothing speedy or 'convenient' about completely healthy cooking. And it's not cheap by the time you have bought herbs, spices and pulses too. Unless of course you are happy with a banana.

More information in my book told me I should be exercising to the point of at least half an hour a day, five times a week. This is no hardship for me, who likes to keep fit, but sometimes there is just no exercising a body that is exhausted from the chemo. I defy anyone to go out for a brisk walk when you can hardly get your head off the pillow. It also persisted in reminding us that positivity is of major support to conquer this disease, and I busied myself with self-hypnosis morning and night, to reinforce the positive thinking. Thus I have managed to avoid the depression of the lack of energy by treating those times as necessary down time to allow the body to heal. Interestingly, when I was on steroids for several days each cycle of chemo, my appetite grew hugely. I just could not stop myself eating. I was like a munching machine. It was hideous! But it did make me realise that in the past when I have treated clients who have been or are on steroids, I was very guilty of thinking, 'pah, that's just an excuse to eat what you like', but believe me it is true. Steriods increase your appetite and it seems nothing will satisfy it. I was out of control with food. It was also interesting that the chemotherapy can have various effects on your food intake because of what it does to all the good cells. For example I found that my taste buds changed so dramatically that even water had a bitter taste. A very strange sensation. It makes me more aware of how important the taste of food is to our consumption of it. Our primary tastes of sweet, salt and bitter dictate to us the main taste, but our numerous taste buds give us the more subtle flavours of our food. When all of these are affected by the chemo, food and drink passing over the taste buds misread the information, more often than not, sending messages to the brain that it tastes shudderingly bad. Once the pleasure of nice taste is gone, the incentive to eat wanes. It is of no surprise that some chemo patients lose weight and even become malnourished because of this. Smells too become more acute and unfortunately not in a nice way. Noises too become louder and one begins to crave quiet. It seems all our senses can be affected quite dramatically.

Even so, I am laid back about it all, taking it in my stride—I know I am lucky. I am supported by a loving husband and family. I try to keep everything in perspective. Yes it's bad, yes it's worrying but I don't have to live every day with the fact that my son died in a motorbike accident two years ago, at 18 years old. My sister does. As they say, you should never have to bury a child. It is the worst imaginable thing to have to face. Jack was the James Dean in the family. Good looking, strong, fun-loving and very popular; and he loved his motorbike. He was going too fast, so the Coroner informed us. The driver didn't see him coming. He was airlifted to hospital but died that day. The shock was immense. The funeral was huge. So many people too, came to pay their respects. Bereavement is a complex procedure. We all pass through the stages and it is quite individual, depending on our relationship with the person, and the people surrounding that person. I was Jack's Auntie, and as such didn't see him very often. A typical teenager, he was working and socialising, if he wasn't in bed. Quite bizarrely, one day I went to my sister's house, and Jack was there watching football on the TV with his dad. They were like brothers they were so close. I hadn't seen Jack for months and months. He was so tall. I tried not to be an old cronie, saying 'My haven't you grown!' Our conversation was light hearted and full of banter. The next day he was dead. To witness such suffering from a close knit family was more that I could hardly bear. Quite how a parent or sibling comes to terms with that I really don't know, nor ever want to, but I will never see a more valiant effort on their part, to hide the immense grief that still goes on in their heart and minds.

Live For The Now

When I see what is going on in the world at this present time, I fear for humanity. The starvation, poverty and disease that countries should have conquered by now, the war in Afghanistan, young soldiers dying . . . mothers' sons; the economy struggling in a world recession; of newsworthy report . . . Amy Winehouse has died at 27 years old of a drugs overdose. She joined the premature death list of Jimmy Hendrix, Janis Joplin, Brian Jones, Jim Morrison and Kurt Cobain who all died at the same age; one hundred youngsters were shot by a possessed maniac wielding a gun in Oslo . . . people's lives changing every day, never to be the same again. An eye opening book about living our lives in the present moment, 'The Power of Now' by Eckhart Tolle, gives us food for thought, about our obsession with the past and the future and not living each day as it comes. Of course we need a life plan, but we spend too much time thinking about the next day, week, month, or year, and don't really experience and 'live' through each day. We are always looking toward the next thing to do, to be or to have. We are never satisfied. We live our lives in the fast lane, and it will be over before we know it, and we won't be able to recreate the memories, because we moved along too fast. Yesterday is gone, tomorrow may never come. I am learning to be more observant of the small things in life which get overlooked, appreciating the natural world more, taking my time, and not getting stressed about doing everything by close of play today.

It brought it home to me that we live in such a materialistic world, when we were packing up our house to move. I realised how much stuff we gather as we go along in life; unnecessary things to spend our money on, cluttering our living space, and leave to gather dust as something new takes its place; so many clothes, shoes, bags and gadgets; so much food in our cupboards and fridges and freezers. Do we think there will be a famine in England? Partly as a result of this, we buy more than we can eat, eat more than our bodies need, and have become very lazy, ever since the days of hunting and gatherings of our ancestors. We live in a disposable world. Nothing is built to last. We don't quite know what to do with all the rubbish we are generating. We are getting better about recycling, but the wasted food mountains are nothing short of criminal. It used to mystify me as a child, when my mother would say, "You are not leaving the table until you have eaten everything on your plate. Just think about those starving children in Africa." My response was often, "Well send it to them then" . . . at least in my head it was. I have learned as a hypnotherapist from clients with weight issues, that for the most part they were made to clear their plates at every meal time through guilt or shame, and the fact that when it is served up to you again for three meals running, there is certain vomit induction going on, and the sure avoidance of that particular food as an adult.

Obesity today is keeping our NHS very busy with bariatric wards springing up in hospitals to keep pace with the ever increasing number of people who are too big to fit into our normal size beds and chairs. This of course has a knock on effect for everything overweight people need or want to do, from getting out of bed and fitting into a normal sized shower or bath, to wanting to go on a joy ride at the theme park, and the seats just aren't big enough. It is difficult to put ourselves into their shoes for a while, and appreciate just how miserable they must be, and how hard that is to cover up and be jolly. And I am betting that not many people go all out to become seriously overweight out of choice. It is more about bad choices, childhood issues, and feeding ourselves to combat negative emotions. I am learning more and more how our state of mind determines our state of body. We get all angry and defensive about our weight too, shouting to whoever will listen that we are being discriminated against because we are fat. It only takes a few rational moments to realise that our bodies aren't meant to be big. We now know the dangers of being seriously overweight; diabetes is at its highest ever levels; strokes, heart attacks and thrombosis too. Our bodies can't cope with heaving all that extra weight around. They weren't designed that way. Take it up with your maker if you have a grievance about it.

The NHS also have the everlasting task of trying to control the numbers of people who are turning to them for diet pills and surgery, and also psychological support as they become depressed and helpless, needing care in the community too, just for basic needs as they become more dependent on others to be looked after.

And after contemplating all of this, we haven't begun to look at all the eating disorders which can overtake people's lives due to the fear of putting on weight, bulimia, anorexia nervosa to name but two. And we don't have far to look to see how these eating disorders can take hold of young minds who are influenced by all they see around them, in magazines, on the television and the internet of how to be the most attractive, how to get the boys, and peer group pressure. We are making our next generation into neurotic waifs who will never appear slim enough to them, and may have a life long struggle with food as a result. Surely, in this day and age, we have a moral obligation to set the appropriate standards to follow, to create a balanced and healthy lifestyle.

Time Is Ticking On

The year is hurrying by. It is already August 2011 and the faint hint of autumn is in the air. I am trying to balance my work and taking care of myself. The chemotherapy exhausts me but I don't let it beat me. It's bizarre how the cancer itself hasn't affected me, but the medical remedy has. I am called to my appointment for more tests to see how I am doing from the inside before my first micro-ablation operation. This is an amazing discovery of surgery, to 'microwave' the tumours to kill them. The following day I was taken in a taxi from the private to the general hospital where they had all the equipment to do this form of surgery, in my operating gown, dressing gown and slippers, and no wig! It felt very odd. When I met my surgeon again, he didn't recognise me without the wig! I am not sure who was more embarrassed. The operation took longer than expected because he found another tumour in the liver behind the first one. He also ablated one tumour each side of the lung. Unfortunately, due to human error, one side was nicked and caused fluid to build on the lung. I woke feeling a whole lot worse as my breathing was impaired. It took a few days for that to clear, and in the meantime I was the proud owner of an antiquated chest drain to carry around the ward with me. For any of you readers who may have had the dubious pleasure of a chest drain, do not read to the end of this paragraph. When it came to the removal of the chest drain, the nurses selectively uninformed me of the excruciating pain I was about to endure, albeit only for a few seconds. When they removed the drain, I let them know I could swear like a guttersnipe. I remembered doing something similar at the birth of my babies, but this exceeded all pain ever experienced before. Why should it be in this day and age, that they can't give you a local anaesthetic for that. Cost I suppose.

As if that wasn't enough, I was in, the following week for the next operation for micro ablation surgery on the other lung. My body was beginning to look like it had bullet holes down my right side! This operation went a lot smoother and I was sent home to recover before the last chemotherapy . . . or so I thought.

Things I Want To Do

People have written books about "50 things to do before I die" and such like. While I had time on my hands, and a lot of thoughts going through my head, I began creating my own 'things I want to do' list. We often say about things we would like to do someday, and someday never comes because we always find something getting in the way of it. Now I am not planning on doing the highest bungee jump in the world, like my daughter did, because that is insanity. I just want to tick some boxes. The first thing was a lazy canal boat trip I had been promising myself for years. It is something pleasurable, tranquil and it was right on top of my list to be done.

The next thing was going to be a bit more costly. It was about July time when I did a lot of thinking about my marriage and how lucky I have been to have a partner who has not left my side through all of this. I wanted to show him how much he meant and continues to mean to me. We had had our first five years of marriage having fun, enjoying life and then had been through a tough five years financially, my ill health, moving house twice, my job at the restaurant going when it closed down, and starting a new business.

I decided as it was our tenth wedding anniversary coming up, to propose we renewed our wedding vows. It would have been a bit of a downer if he had said no, but he said yes it was a brilliant idea. This gave us a great emotional boost as we planned a really lovely day. Optimism and positivity are crucial to maintaining wellbeing and control.

With plans for the Vows day well under way, I thought about other things I would like to do, and I'm sure it's the kind of normal little adventures we all would like to enjoy, have a powerboat race, stay in a little cottage overlooking a vast expanse of shimmering sea, go and see a show, visit Scotland, nothing extraordinary, but just for me; perhaps a few city breaks, taking up dancing, the list goes on and on.

More Bad News

Truth to tell, we don't know what is going on inside our bodies. By now it is mid-October and I have another scan with the radiologist who did the ablation surgery. I began to feel all was not good, as he took so long to call us in. It was bad news. He told me there were lots of little tumours growing on my lung and liver. I was so shocked. Only the week before my oncologist said my Xray was fine. Back to the oncologist I went, fearing the worst now. Nothing prepares you for news like this. He decided more chemotherapy of the tablet variety plus an antibody infusion every three weeks for 6 cycles. At this point my husband and I decided to seek a second opinion and asked for a referral to The Royal Marsden in London, one of the five hospitals in the world specialising in cancer. We went up by train, and took a taxi to the hospital in Chelsea. We had always gone to London on the train when we were having a jolly day out, but it wasn't a pleasurable trip this time. The consultant agreed with my oncologist as to the next treatment to try, so that reassured us he was on the right track.

Following this, we decided to take off for a few days to Cornwall with our dogs to make a break from the constant round of hospital visits, and be normal. It did us the world of good. I came back fired up and ready to face my demons. I needed to pull out all of the stops and do my damnedest to make this go away. I reread the Anticancer book and absorbed more information about what I might be doing which wasn't helping. I had been a bit too relaxed about the food I was eating, and realised I would have to radically adjust my diet—back to basics for cooking.

When I started chemo 5 years ago, I decided that for every horrible session I had, I would treat myself. I was having a lot of treats by now! My wardrobe was gradually being replaced, as were shoes and bags. Now it was time for a new wig! With my Vows day looming, I wanted hair that had movement. My sister drove me to the wig shop, where they assist people to find a suitable natural looking wig. It was hysterical. You can be anyone you want to be with a new wig. I finally settled on one which was not too outrageous and rather looked like my hair used to be before I lost it all. It gives you a huge confidence boost when your 'hair' looks good. I thought I would test it out at my 'hen' night . . . or maybe that should be 'chicken' night. Twenty of us dressed up as Flapper girls in 1920s Charleston style dresses, beads and feathers. It was a psychological success for me, catapulting me into thoughts of total positivity. I would not be beaten by this disease.

Let The
Battle Commence

Well they tried to get a canula into my poor battered, damaged collapsed veins to deliver the antibody treatment, but it left my hand and arm bruised and sore. They wouldn't use the right arm at all following the removal of all the lymph glands. This was clearly not going to work for another five treatments plus blood tests etc. So my only option was to have a portcath fitted. This is something placed under the skin with a line into a vein, to enable the drugs to enter the body. The choice was arm or chest. I opted for the chest not really appreciating how visible it would be. I didn't relish the idea of another operation just for this but had little choice. Back into hospital for a general anaesthetic and a 45 minute operation. I was surprised it took a while to recover just from that, and that was before the next lots of treatment. It seemed never ending.

In the meantime more treats for me. We carried on as normal. Christmas was coming, and all that entailed kept

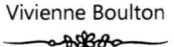
me busy. We went to a Charity Ball, so I had a new dress. We went to London to see a show, eat out and forget for a bit, and life carried on all around us; we made times of fun and enjoyment, in-between the horrible bits.

Vows Day

*I*t was December 8th 2011, our tenth wedding anniversary. We had planned a special day to mark the occasion. I was lucky to have got to this day, after my very dodgy start to the year. But I never had any doubts it would be a wonderful day. I had to have chemo three days before this day, and was in a state because I had a rash come up over my neck and chest. What timing! It was angry and bright red. Lovely. I rubbed anticeptic cream in that rash day and night, and on the morning I just about got away with it. It is so important to feel right at any stage of treatment. Positivity is the key word. Wellbeing is another. If I could have bottled all the good feelings in the room on that day, it would serve me well for a very long time. We wrote our vows to say to each other, and our lovely friend Ruediger said a few words at the ceremony, which was touching, so kind, and heart felt. Everything about the day was about us. Even the cake had "drunken bride and groom" lying on it, surrounded by empty bottles of champagne!

We took ourselves off to Brighton for the weekend, in celebration, to a hotel we thought would be fitting for a "honeymoon" night, however it turned out to be something like Fawlty Towers! We found it all rather amusing, and it didn't detract from a fun weekend, out to dinner and Jools Holland in concert. We raced home on the Sunday morning in readiness for more celebrations with the family.

We traditionally had Xmas Sunday lunch for my siblings and partners, in the week before Christmas at my younger sister's house. It was so lovely. Such a closeness, and optimism and hope for the future for all of us. We had all the traditional trimming, with crackers, secret Santa presents, and lots of food and drink. These occasions become more and more precious.

Munich In The Snow

This was to be a big adventure. We hadn't been abroad for a few years, and were excited to be going away for a few days with friends, to a new country for us. There was just one small issue that raised its head when we flew abroad. We both had flight phobia. For myself I had 'talked' myself down to a much more rational way of dealing with it, especially after everything I had been through, but my husband still panicked at the thought of being shut in, out of control of the plane himself—thank God he wasn't flying it!—and proceeded to get very drunk in order to catch the flight. He was certainly feeling no pain when we boarded, and was a very well behaved drunk, so no one knew.

Munich was everything we expected and more. A rich city, Munich offered us a different culture to explore, with traditional Christmas markets, Gluehwein to drink outside in the cold snowy parks; fabulous sights of the Alps, and castles, small villages steeped in history. Munich is full of expensive shops; it is a wealthy city. It is also a city of great emotion; a fire burns continually in a monolith, in memory of the atrocities and shame for the innocent people who died in the Second World War. There are still lives affected by that period. It was snowy and so pretty. Other countries are so much better at dealing with snowy conditions, compared to us Brits. Our country comes to a standstill very quickly at the first fall. However it was nothing for Munich to handle. Having said that this was remarkably the coldest winter Europe had endured for 25 years.

Back from Munich and straight into Christmas, we carried on with all of our plans which we had made a few months ago, at the time thinking I would be over all hospital visits, fighting fit and having fun. I managed to continue with my treatments. The tablet form of chemotherapy suited me, and side effects were minimal. On Christmas Eve I went to church with my two younger sisters. We are not sure why we do this every year; it takes us back to our roots I suppose. When we were young that is what we did, albeit on Christmas morning then, before the grand opening of presents. If we didn't go to church every Sunday ordinarily, the nuns at school would find out, because they would ask us what the sermon had been about. No pressure. I did attempt to make it up a few times, knowing the nuns wouldn't have been to the little church where I lived, but it was too scary. They could see right through me to my soul, or so I believed. We nicknamed our head nun 'the poisonous penguin' because to us, she was indeed, small and deadly! She was very short and round with horn-rimmed glasses, and as she crept around the school in her flat black shoes, we lived in fear of her waiting to pounce. I recall once, at the grown up age of 11, a few of us going round the back of the bike sheds to read a book, which was an eye opening novel for our naïve class, called 'Here We Go Round The Mulberry Bush.' It had a racy paragraph or two in it of lovers entwined and we had just got to the good bit, when we heard a sudden roar . . . "What are you girls reading?" We all got the ruler across the back of our hands for that, and detentions of course. We were sure she had a good time checking the book out in her study afterwards.

As our children grew, we would take them to the teddy bears service on Christmas Eve, with their grandmothers. When the grandmothers died, and the children grew up, we just kept on going. It was poignant to hear the church organ belting out the carols, creating a huge swell of sound and emotion, and it reminded us of course of our dad. It also served a purpose of our sister who had lost her son, as she felt closer to him on those occasions, although sometimes the emotion was too much to bear, and we left before the end.

It's interesting how deep-seated our roots are, and how much of what we learn in childhood, good or bad, stays with us into adulthood, and forms our critical belief system which we find extraordinarily difficult to change on a conscious level. I have treated many clients whose childhoods have marred their normal development into adulthood, and coloured their judgement until they could no longer cope or stand it, and finally sought help. Abusive, disciplinarian, cold and unloving, uncaring parenting creates mentally scarred children, whose relationships suffer a great deal as a result. How cruel to subject your child to emotional harm. We say children are resilient; 'oh they will be alright' . . . but everything is absorbed by our subconscious minds and if it's bad, we lock it away to save more hurt, and that too becomes destructive. We all need to feel love and be loved.

Love is crucial to our well-being. Lack of love brings fear, resentment, insecurity and instability, which we end up searching for, for the rest of our lives. Now I know not all children are loveable beings. They can test the most even person's temper at times, but children aren't born bad. They become products of their environment. And they don't come with an instruction manual. We have to learn how to bring up children, using our own best judgment, skills and love. Sometimes people who have had a harsh upbringing say 'I don't want that to happen to my child', but we are conditioned by our own experiences, and often history repeats itself. If we see the parents drinking heavily, or eating vast amounts of food, or we get beaten or abused, this is acceptable because the people we trust most are doing it, so it must be ok. But as we grow and learn what is and is not acceptable, we must then decide for ourselves what is right and wrong. Some of us have hard lessons to learn in life through no fault of our own, and we should respect and acknowledge our good judgements, praise ourselves for our courage and determination to have a better life, and especially to nurture little human beings to become the best possible adults they can be. We don't appreciate how precious a commodity life is, until it is threatened.

We decided to have the alternative Christmas Day and take my girls out for a curry! As roast dinner is not their favourite food, it made sense to cut out the work and enjoy being cooked for! Whilst all around us, families were busily basting turkeys, we only had ourselves to please. Having done all the family visitations before Christmas, it was the perfect solution. And surprisingly a lot of others had the same idea! This idea is really catching on. We relaxed into the next few days, eating and drinking, putting the world behind us.

Boxing day is traditionally a day when all of our surrounding villages converge to have the famous 'Pram Race'. Now as you might suspect, prams are becoming more and more scarce, with buggies taking over the world, so there are variations on a theme allowed these days. Fancy Dress is a must for all the entrants, as is partaking of a pint of freezing cold beer outside every pub the race passes. At 11am on a cold and frosty December day, this is a daunting task. Adaptions of prams arrive with wheels fixed on rods to frames to make huge topical fancy dress entries. For days afterwards our local village is strewn with abandoned prams in a state of collapse, buckled and bent beyond recognition, which is no surprise, when the 'baby' can weigh 18 stones! For years our family have had one or two members enter the Pram Race, I even did it myself with Roger a few years ago. We entered, dressed as Kat and Alfi Slater from Eastenders. It was hysterical. Oh for the days of carefree enjoyment again.

The Pram Race is a great time for meeting up with friends old and new who you don't see from one year to the next otherwise. I have always found it amazing that we live so close to people who we never bump into. We have indeed become an insular society. What I liked about this day was my anonymity. No one knew about my illness, so I was treated normally. People often don't seem to know how to behave around illness and either stare at you warily, or fawn over you like long lost friends who actually haven't bothered you for years, or they cross over the road so as to avoid any conversation at all. I know because I have done it myself. We struggle to deal with illness. We struggle to deal with death. When we meet and greet we say "How are you?" not really wanting to know how they actually are! We expect a "I'm fine thank you." and quickly move on. And if someone is determined to tell us how they really are, we are horrified at the amount of information that is suddenly passed on without hardly a 'by your leave!' Truth to tell we really don't want to know. It's almost as if, if we aren't told, then it can't happen to us. Our brains are like sponges and absorb information, assimilate it, copy it. Some people are particularly susceptible and become hypochondriac, firmly believing they have immediately contracted the disease merely by talking to this person. What a miserable life they must lead. State of mind is everything, and once we realise we can make changes for a more positive and successful future we improve our lives tremendously; and everyone else's around us who has to put up with all the moaning and groaning. We only have to want it, to make it happen.

As the year draws to a close, New Year's Eve beckons, with the promise of a better new year. Some have cause to celebrate the end of a good year, others cause to celebrate the end of a bad year, glad that it's over and done, looking forward to improvement with hope and optimism. New Year's Eve can often be a disappointing evening in itself. We tend to hold so much store in it being the most brilliant night, leading the way to a brilliant new year, but so often it falls flat, and we are left feeling deflated before we have even started January. Well I for once was looking forward to the end of 2011. It had been the worst year of my life, and I looked forward with strength and determination to make my future all I wanted it to be. We shared a lovely evening with our fabulous friends Jeannette, Ruediger and others at their home, and vowed 2012 was going to be our year.

Another New Year

When the fun is done, and it's back to the grind, it's cold, dark and dank outside, we've spent up, pigged out, and face the consequences of overindulging over the Yuletide, we sink into a low mood, head hung down, battling with a very long January. But I had no time to waste. There were changes happening. January 4th 2012, exactly a year to the day we started our Therapy Centre for Hypnotherapy and Counselling, Jeannette informed me that the business could no longer sustain the losses we were making and as financial director of the company, she would have no choice but to close our business down by the end of June 2012. Well this wasn't a surprise to me, although it was a concrete blow to us. The figures didn't lie. We were running at a loss. The overheads were too high. There are thousands of people out there who would benefit hugely from our services, but they weren't coming for help. Financially our country, along with many others, was deep in recession, with no near end to it. In more lenient times, we would have managed to get our business off and running successfully, but the odds were stacked against us. I could hold my head up and know I did not stop working throughout that whole year. I sometimes felt so tired, but I carried on for my clients' sake, and for the business. We so wanted it to work. We had tried everything we could think of. We had advertised in numerous ways, local radio, hospital information boards, hand delivered leaflets, newspaper features, local shops boards, and car adverts. But people were being very cautious with their money. We even tried discounting our fees, but it was having no effect. It was so disappointing when we knew how much difference these therapies make to people. We knew it worked. Time and time again we had success with weight control, stop smoking, controlling your illness, and major issues such as anxiety, fears and phobias. Problems which were overwhelming getting back under control. What is so upsetting is the lack of attention the NHS was paying to alternative therapies and their place in our society. Our medical world thrives off the latest pills, surgery and treatment, endorsed by all the medical practitioners who would be without a job if they didn't. All the medical companies who produce all of the pills, surgical implements etc, suppliers for doctors, surgeries and hospitals are paid to sustain the belief that the only way to good health is through the medical channels. It's what makes the world go around. What is very worrying is the current pressure on our NHS to make financial cuts, leaving patients without treatment, according to where they live, and the NHS budgets in their area. It is astonishing, ludicrous and appalling.

However, it would be hard to ignore how well our bodies can look after themselves using the energy, and genes within us. For thousands of years, our good health has been guided by religious beliefs, prayer, meditation and lifestyle. We have lost the belief in ourselves. My dear friend discovered another book 'The Genie in our Genes' by Dawson Church PhD, Epigenetic

Medicine and the New Biology of Intention. It unfolds and explains the powers of epigenetics. Essentially we are only just beginning to work out how complicated the superstructure of our bodies are and what they are capable of.

So many times I hear of people diagnosed with a serious disease, and before long they have given up, given in to it, and die. Where has all the fight gone in us, our survival instinct? Is it that we really don't care anymore about life and living? There is nothing more precious than life and we owe it to ourselves to live our lives to the full, give it as much meaning as possible. And appreciate all the life around us.

Twists And Turns

January trickles on in a haze of cold damp miserableness. I actually felt fine. I was coping admirably with my latest chemo and antibody treatment and I had got to the half way mark, when the next scan was due. I was feeling rather buoyant in fact. I even took myself back to the gym for the first time in a year. I was determined to get fit again, and being appreciative of life, dog walking, observing nature, taking time, practising what I preach. I was also determined to get my driving licence back again after a year. I was still so angry about the withdrawal of my licence on a general rule of thumb for 'people who have had a brain tumour'. Ban them ban them, they may be a danger to us all. Yes well I think we only have to look around us to know there are many, many more dangers on the roads in the form of useless careless drivers! I would like to have the people who made that decision for me wear my shoes for a year and see how they like the injustice of it! We don't realise just how much we depend on our trusty vehicles. We have become a society who no longer lives and works and dies in the village and the community. We live a distance from our work, the shops, our families too. Because we can get into our cars and go there. Travel is not an issue any more. Unless you haven't got a car. It is as natural to take driving lessons at 17 years old, as it is to take A levels. We have to do it because everyone else is doing it. We look with surprise if someone says they don't drive. We immediately think there must be something wrong with them. Or they are just plain thick. It doesn't matter that at 17 we are probably at quite a vulnerable stage in life, fairly irresponsible, self-centred, financially dependent and most likely to prang the new love of our life within a month of having it! But nevertheless more and more cars are on the road every day, bringing traffic chaos to us with no end in sight, only worse to come.

Well, as is becoming the norm, my scan results were not good. Another shock. My oncologist tells me there are more liver tumours. This latest treatment has been doing no good. The lung tumours have stayed pretty much the same, which whilst not great wasn't awful, but the liver tumours have multiplied. What is going on? Why isn't the medical treatment or indeed my own self-healing working? Now things are getting pretty nasty. I am getting very angry that nothing is working. I fully intend to be completely well this year, so now the time has come. The oncologist has decided I must change treatment to the conventional form of chemotherapy again with two new drugs, plus a top up of one of the drugs the following week.

It's February and we begin again, with longer durations at the hospital for the administration of the drugs. And I am back on the steroids. Now I am really angry. I have played the game, put up with all the crap, and still I am not out of the woods. There must be a way of getting my body to heal itself. It does it all the time when we cut our finger, or strain a muscle. Why should cancer be any different. It is after all my cells which have gone awry, so I should be able to make those cells get back in line. Having read more books on the discovery of making oneself well again, I was guided by a book called 'Getting Well Again' by O. Carl Simonton M.D. It incorporates all I have learned about using hypnosis and the power of your mind, and using your inner guide to get your body back on track, looking after itself. Now this can mean anything which you can relate to in terms of innermost self, be it your sub-conscious, your unconscious self, your God, or some other serious figure with a great deal of symbolic value.

This brings me back to religion which forms our beliefs and allows us to believe, trust and hope in a higher being to support us in our present life and the hereafter. For some this means there is no doubt that although our physical life ends on this earth, our souls go on and we are answerable to every misdemeanour we have ever made. From Buddhism to Christianity, Hinduism to Islam, religion essentially means a higher way of living; a more respectful, altruistic, kind, meaningful way of being. Unfortunately our world has always had dark places of religious unrest, which has led to warring factions since time began. But essentially here we are looking at praying to a Higher Being for guidance and strength, to be led away from discord, and into a happier state of mind and body. Our inner mind controls our body; our subconscious mind always has the power over our conscious mind. And so I set about changing some of the beliefs I had held onto for so long, which I came to realize were preventing me from allowing my body to heal. Because we can have long held beliefs which we are using as a weapon to actually promote illness in ourselves, and to hold onto that illness as it can be a way of not facing reality.

I began to look at what may have triggered this disease in me. O. Carl Simonton suggests there is a possible window of about six to eighteen months before the onset of cancer, when huge stress factors can be responsible for adversely affecting our immune system, which normally keeps us fit and healthy. Looking back there have been a number of stressful events which have probably contributed to my poor health, both created as a result of my own inner beliefs and those events out of my control. It is significant how many people are affected by stress and how damaging it can be. And it's not so much the actual stress, rather how we do or do not deal with it that matters. When we internalise, and bury the stress, we are putting our body under such pressure, our health declines. I know I am guilty of trying to "make everything right" for everyone, to the detriment of myself. I believe my mother was just the same. She died of throat cancer. I think she had given up really. She didn't seem to have anything to live for, once we five children had left home, and my dad had died. She had devoted her life to caring for her family and working, and once retired and alone, there seemed nothing much to carry on for. She didn't have any hobbies or pastimes, always too busy for that. I seem to be guilty of the same. I even resented Roger's laissez faire attitude. I felt everyone should be working all of the time for the good of all, from morning till night. I felt responsible to keep everything together. I put such pressure on myself I made myself ill. I certainly didn't wish to have cancer, but in a way it had been serving me a purpose. I must stop making myself responsible for events out of my control. I could now stop blaming myself, being resentful, because I had to have all of this treatment. I came to realise that I was using the cancer as an excuse not to deal with my negative beliefs, and change myself for my own good. I am

sometimes described as 'the kindest person in the world'. This means I always put everyone else before myself. I am guilty of that. And I resent people who do put themselves first, hugely! But I lost myself somewhere along the way. Now I am beginning to find myself in all of this. I can understand more about myself.

Chemotherapy begins again. A dual chemotherapy this time. The side effects for me are minimal. Day 8 goes ok too, a top up of one of the drugs, and February passes uneventfully, as I wade through the treacle that is chemotherapy. Into March and working hard on my self-hypnosis. More books from Jeannette arrive, about Epigenetics, all about how we can change our genetic makeup, and a spiritual awakening through her oracle cards. She gave me a copy of the card she turned over for me, and it was the Mother Mary, saying Mary had heard me and a miracle is coming. Up until then, I hadn't given much thought to my spiritual side. This struck a chord and I began visualizing a miracle of perfect health. I read book after book about events which had happened in other peoples' lives, ('Quantum Change' by William R. Miller and Janet C'de Baca; 'Love medicine and Miracles' by Bernie Siegal to name but two) and it made more and more sense. I began to believe in a higher power which could create this miracle in me. Miracles do happen. My certainty of getting rid of the cancer grew stronger and stronger.

All the efforts I was making and the chemotherapy, along with such support from my family and friends of prayers, energy and love, surely couldn't fail.

Changes
Are Happening

Wednesday 28th March 2012 was a momentous day for me, and this might seem trivial in the scheme of things, but I was told I could drive again . . . . legally. What a joy and freedom again! I had persecuted the DLVA for the last six weeks, trying to hurry things along. They were becoming as exasperated with me as I was with them. They said 'we are very busy you know; lots of people want their driving licence back', to which I retorted 'well if you weren't so keen to stop everyone driving with your blanket rule of if there is a diagnosis of a brain tumour the licence is withdrawn for at least a year, without considering reports from surgeons saying this person is fine to drive, then you wouldn't have so much paperwork to process when it came to renewing the licence!' I felt better for having aired my opinion but it wasn't getting me any nearer. I was then told that I did not meet the criteria for jumping the queue, so I politely asked what that criteria was. I was told if the licence was needed for work I would be put at the front of the queue. Well I have had clients in the past who needed me to treat them in their home, and after my explanation that I had clients waiting for treatment pending, hey presto, my application was examined and two days later I got my driving licence back. I think they were quite glad to see the back of me! And cancer patients are supposed to live stress-free lives. This doesn't help.

My partner had decided enough was enough and we had to close the Therapy Centre. The overheads were too high for the amount of clients we were getting. We spent the week selling off the furniture and for me, finding different treatment rooms. It was rather sad to think only fifteen months ago we were so ready to make a success of this business. My illness had lasted the whole of that time, but I never stopped working. We gave it our all. Now it was time for change again.

I had an interesting client return to me after a period of time, although not for the same issue. She had come to me originally for treatment for IBS, stress and panic attacks. She was a good subject for hypnotherapy. After a few sessions, her IBS was under control, she had stopped having panic attacks and she was controlling her stress levels. Her sessions were going well. She discovered she was pregnant and became anxious about the birth. I gave her four sessions on hypno-birthing, and despite an emergency Caesarean Section, she coped admirably. She contacted me again after four months in a sad state with post natal depression. She came to her first session weeping, and went home a changed woman. She had one more session and was fine, enjoying her baby. She even came back for some weight loss sessions. What an amazing therapeutic tool hypnosis is. It can literally change your life.

It was by now the end of March and time for my mid treatment CT scan. I felt very apprehensive about the results. Well who wouldn't after what had gone before. I was getting used to these scans by now. A few days later the results were in. The drive to the hospital was quiet. Roger and I did not speak much. Spring was all around us, everything bursting into life but I didn't notice it as we travelled through the countryside to the hospital. It's interesting watching people in these waiting rooms. Half of them, including me, have a magazine in front of them, and turn the pages without reading anything, their minds turning over the possible outcomes of their appointment to come. When my name was called, we took a deep breath and went in. My oncologist was smiling. He rarely smiles . . . The CT scan showed the tumours had shrunk considerably. The first bit of good news in fifteen months. Whatever I was or was not doing was working. My oncologist believed it was the chemotherapy at last. My sister believed it was her prayers being answered. My friend believed it was the positive energy she was sending, and her spiritual influences. I believed it was my hypnotherapy, positive beliefs, fitness, diet and everything else which couldn't fail to beat this cancer. Whatever it was I ordered more of the same!

And so the rolling programme continued. The chemicals in the chemotherapy also continued to upset my normal body functions. My blood count was down, and my oncologist decided that even though I was a tough old bird, he declined me having the back up chemo on day 8. This time it was the red blood cells not recovering. I was now concerned with not having the treatment, more put out that I had wasted more than half a day at the hospital. Something inside me had definitely changed. I was forward thinking, making the most of every day, and every experience, living in the now.

Time for another fun break away in the caravan! March this year had been unusually warm, hot even at times. It had spoilt us for what was to become the wettest April for 20 odd years! We set off with great hopes of a change in the weather, to a site only an hour and a half from home. Mud mud mud, torrential downpours and BBQing in the hailstones. It was an experience not to be repeated in a hurry! I am a miserable person if I am cold, and sat, grimfaced in the caravan with the cooker on full pelt. Now, one has to ask oneself the question, what are we doing here? And it's funny how the other 'holidaymakers' seemed to be so much less muddy than us! Of course the nicest day was when we packed up to come home. However it did take me out of myself and I stopped thinking about my health. Getting a break in the mental confusion of life is very beneficial. I have to admit to getting rather fractious when it came to making the bed up every night, constructing it from all of the caravan seats was a jigsaw puzzle, followed by a very stubborn fitted sheet which refused to stay on all four corners of the 'bed'. I threw all my toys out of the pram and called Roger in to use brute strength on it, and we flopped on the bed exhausted. The dogs proceeded to put muddy pawprints onto the clean bedding as they climbed up to get in on the act before we could stop them, and I decided from then on, I am a fair weather camper only!

Back to work, always occupying myself with helping others where ever my skills were needed, I was having a number of clients contacting me for the hypnotic gastric band treatment. This is an amazing form of hypnotherapy which convinces the client, he or she has had surgery to reduce the size of the stomach, and hence, can only eat small portions of food. Some analysts of this psychotherapy say this takes away the responsibility of the client to control their food consumption, but I say if they cannot stop eating, and it is harming them, it is a control measure which will greatly help create a better lifestyle change. It empowers them rather than disempowers them, and unlike the actual surgery which isn't easily reversible, it is reversible. Hypnotherapy also changes the way they think about food, and address the emotional issues concerned with why they use food to satisfy emotions and feelings other than hunger. This is why so many people put the weight back on after dieting with Slimming World and Weightwatchers. They go back to the old ways of eating and just pile it all back on. Yo-Yo dieting as it is affectionately known, is a way of life for some. Getting back the control is so important for self-esteem and confidence. Success in life makes us proud and triggers more success. Quite often, weight issues stem from childhood, being overfed or underfed, not being fed healthily due to lack of knowledge about food, cost, parental control . . . remember ? "You will not leave this table until you clear your plate". "There are children in Africa starving while you are wasting food." Sometimes our parents don't get it right. Sometimes they themselves are suffering from eating disorders created by their upbringing. It takes a very strong child to see it's mother eating then vomiting (Bulimia) and not get an eating disorder of their own.

I am off my soapbox now, and busy working. I was taught to use any aid I could to make the hypnotic gastric band session as realistic as possible with the help of a pretend injection of anaesthetic, the smell of surgical spirit, and hospital sounds.

I was having problems with my computer and decided it would be best to download the hospital sounds I had onto my ipod. Well not being the most technical minded, I truly believed I had replicated what was on my computer. I must admit I was rather apprehensive with my first client following this change of delivery, and was half way through her session, and started playing the tracks. All was going well until the ipod jumped into TRex, Hot Love! Thinking fast, I explained to the client that the surgeon was at ease with his work, and was enjoying his music while he operated! Phew! It didn't detract from her most important session and she went on to lose 4 stones in weight.

Well I am getting through my chemotherapy now. Session 5 was upon me before I knew it, and off I went to spend the day at the hospital. I have been lucky enough to be treated privately, and this provides an element of being in a hotel. I am offered tea, coffee and biscuits on arrival, swiftly followed by ordering lunch from a rather good menu. There is a healthy option always, but who chooses that on a day when you just want lots of comfort? Bad foods such as deep fried scampi and chips, sponge pudding and custard was the order of the day, and I even ate all the biscuits while I was there! Resistance to such temptation was low if not non-existent, and I stuffed myself with bread as well. It goes to show, if you are a captive audience, and you tell yourself in hypnosis, you do not feel sick and everything tastes good, it does, and with the steroids doing a damn good job of increasing my appetite ten-fold, I was fast becoming a very rotund person—not a good example to my clients who come for weight control.

On a more serious note, having cancer changes your life, of that there is no doubt. Not only does the disease control your life, it has an effect on lifestyle too. The treatments, constant to and fro to the hospital, recovery time etc all have an effect on day to day living, not least trying to hold down a job while all of this is going on. Money doesn't necessarily make you happy, but it certainly helps . . . as the saying goes. For so many of us, we worry about lack of money. It compounds what is already a traumatic time, when we can't make ends meet. Some of us are lucky enough to have partners and family to lean on. When cancer strikes, all our energy and strength is required to help us heal. In the western world, we do not suffer so greatly from lack of food and shelter, but living costs are for ever rising. I had a tough time financially throughout my life with cancer. Keeping positive about everything was life's biggest challenge for me. But this is what we must do. Using every means available to instil hope for good health, prosperity and longevity kept me going throughout my illness. And now I was at the end of my journey with cancer. I no longer wanted or needed it. It was time for it to leave.

I am unfortunate enough to not have the strongest of teeth along with some of my siblings, a legacy from my father. Between us we have kept dentists in plush Mercedes for many a year! Actually my eldest sister opted to privately pay for implants to replace her steadily decreasing number of teeth. Now when people start talking about their experiences and pain from the dentist we all seem to glaze over with boredom as it seems people take great delight in recounting every detail . . . as though it is interesting to anyone else. Suffice to say I had to have a tooth extracted the day after Chemo number 6, which for two weeks compounded my misery. It's hard to suck chicken enough in order to swallow it, and as for anything that needed chewing more than four times, forget it. My smile, when I actually felt like smiling, was becoming rather bereft of teeth. Not a pretty sight. I would be organising a big treat for myself very shortly for enduring this round of treatment,

To distract myself I decided we should go to the cinema. There was apparently a particularly funny film showing locally, so off we went to eat first, something we didn't do much so rather a novelty. I managed to give myself severe indigestion from lack of chewing my chicken enough to break it down, however I was determined to eat it. We had decided, Roger and I, not to buy the exorbitantly priced sweets these multiplex cinemas sell. We know it is rubbish; we know it is expensive, but do we listen to ourselves? Roger's resolve was gone immediately he saw all the sweets on display, with shovels and bags just begging to be picked up and filled. Who pays £11.95 for a heap of sugar? We did. We shouldn't eat it, and we could both do without the empty calories, not to mention the sugar rotting our teeth, what's left of them, but that mattered not a jot. We busily munched our way through the lot before the film had hardly begun. Guilt crept in immediately, but I figured everyone deserved to break the rules now and again. It seems everywhere you go, there are temptations to break our rules to eat healthily. I didn't see any fruit for sale in the Cinema, just sweets, nachos and hotdogs.

We are conditioned by what we see. There is not much point in advertising food on the radio, but television and magazines have a very powerful impact on our subconscious because we are suggestible, living in a 'see it, must have it' world. The supermarkets where many of us shop regularly work very hard and spend enormous amounts of money encouraging us to eat. They encourage us to drink alcohol too with offers too good to pass up. Fast food outlets are everywhere offering us calorific takeaways to satiate our ever increasing appetites. You only have to stand in London Victoria Railway station and watch as people are constantly buying food on the go. There are more cookery programmes on the television than ever before making us feel hungry watching them, even if we have just eaten. Is it any wonder the Western world now has staggering statistics of obesity, and as a consequence ill-health.

There is a lot we can do for ourselves so we don't fall into the traps laid down for us. Being aware of exactly what we are consuming is a good start. Knowledge of what a healthy diet is and portion size is crucial. In my years as a hypnotherapist I have discovered some very bizarre eating habits. We are responsible for ourselves and should be taking back the control over our own bodies.

When I walk down the road I see more fat people than normal people. I whisper under my breath "hypnotic gastric band, hypnotic gastric band", hoping their subconscious minds will register this, and find professional therapists to get them on the road to recovery. It's time to stop blaming everyone and everything else for what we become, and take control.

Chemo 6 done and back-up session of drugs done, I have a CT scan to see where I am now. My oncologist smiles once again as I walk in the door of his consulting room for the results. As said before . . . he rarely smiles. The news is good. The lung tumours are inactive and the liver tumours have shrunk considerably again! A huge sigh of relief and it takes a while to sink in. I am told I can have a three months break to enjoy the summer which turns out to be the wettest ever. No matter though, the future is looking long healthy and happy and that's good enough for me!

My advice to anyone who has to embark on a journey with cancer is to always have a positive mind. Accept the medical treatment and tell yourself you are happy to have it. Use your subconscious mind to control and eradicate the disease. Get rid of any stress holding you back, using positive attitude, self-belief, self-talk, and your spirituality. Enjoy every day of your life in any way you can. Life is precious. Let's make the most of it.

The Future

The way I see it, I will live into my eighties; I picture myself sitting in an armchair with my grand-children around me, happy and smiling. It's all about keeping one step ahead of the game. I am told that if the cancer should become active again, there are still treatments I haven't tried. I do not consider requiring those treatments.

Having had breast cancer, secondary cancer in the brain, liver and lung, and beaten it, I consider myself quite an expert on the subject. I would rather not be, but having lived through it and experienced some of what my clients have experienced or are experiencing, I can honestly say it has made me a better person. I am lucky.

In Passing

*A*t half-past midnight on 3rd December 2012 my beautiful, inspirational wife and best friend Vivienne slipped peacefully away, held gently in my arms and in the loving presence of her three daughters, Katie, Charlotte and Kelsey and her brother Martin.

In the four months from completion of her story to her passing, Viv never at any stage accepted that she wouldn't make it, live to see her eventual grandchildren, party-on with me into the autumn and winter of her life. Her every-day positive affirmations and self-hypnosis regime could arguably be credited with prolonging her life, it is indisputable that the quality and joy of her remaining time with me was above all normal expectations as a direct consequence. She had no fear, no pain, she remained at home with me throughout. The self-help program of hypnosis and positive thinking that she so enthusiastically and successfully espoused for her clients, she in turn fully embraced for herself. It made the difference.

The last words of her story testify that "I am lucky". Well my darling, as you kept telling me throughout our fairy-tale, wonderful life and love together, it was I that was the lucky one. Lucky to know you, laugh with you, dance with you, love you so very dearly, have your warm, generous and total love in return.

Sleep well my Vivacious Viv, see you in a while . . . .

Lightning Source UK Ltd.
Milton Keynes UK
UKOW03f2214010514

230985UK00001B/3/P